Mad God's Love (Romance)

Hazel Young

Contents

Chapter One

CHAPTER 1

A demon stroked girl's hair with an unbecoming gentleness and her body slumped down like an open bag of potatoes, with about as much life left in her too. All that chirpy energy snuffed out like an afterthought. That's what they did. The demons. It was beyond obvious, even if one wasn't exposed to continuous preaching about it. There was no way to miss it either figure carried massive horns on his hooded head. She was the fool to approach one. Trust him.

I could not help but snort in my amusement. He had to have known I was already here anyway and I was not going to miss out on my last remaining laugh. There's not been many occasions for that before. Even before these creatures flooded the world. I almost want to say it was an improvement, but was too tired for spite.

Figure didn't look up or look around. "I did not expect another happy fool," a scratchy boom carried well from afar. Too well. I shouldn't have heard it. Definitely didn't when the odd pair sauntered in chattering amongst themselves. It was distinctly inhuman cadence. "Or are you gleeful psychopath about to offer me a job?"

As I was too tired to shout, muttered to mostly to myself, "Why, you short on cash or something?" Me too, buddy. I wouldn't be here if I had had any to spare. Who knew, money made two worlds spin.

I probably shouldn't have been surprised, but he'd heard me again. "Are you really trying to bribe me?" all-too-low rumble made me shudder with cold.

Was his own dumb idea, but who was I to argue with ancient evil? Patted myself over, winced and spoke out loud with actual intention to be heard, "Sorry, my wallet must be in some other pants." Which was true, in a sense. I was alright with my hands and my fingers would stick to things if there was a chance. "Do you take cheques?" Or I could definitely do an IOU. Especially since I wouldn't be expected to pay anything back in my short remaining life. Hell, maybe he was even serious? I could definitely sic this preternatural evil upon a few people. Highly doubtful, as that would mean my luck wasn't completely rotten.

"I don't much care for your overvalued paper," he'd eventually spoken and I pinned distaste on the bland tone for my own state of mind.

"Hey they're usually like... fabric or even plastic," I came to an unexpected defence of our financial institution. Hell, not even I cared about this.

But fair point. What did the horrors use as a currency? I looked at the untouched corpse at his feet. Which was weird in itself weren't the beasts supposed to devour their prey? Come to think of it, wasn't it strange to find one that was talking too?

Instead of taking the bait as a normal human being - which of course he wasn't the demon seemed to have grown tired of the exchange entirely. The deep reverberating rumble chilled me more than the stone I was lounging on as he decreed, "You reek of death so you're capable of seeing to your affairs."

I shuddered for a slew of reasons. He'd just leave me here. "Do you uh... want a soul? As a... payment."

He moved for the first time since we've spoken, just to cross arms at his chest and look extra smug with his horned head finally turning as though for my benefit. Because the gesture certainly wasn't innate to a foreign entity who moved just to get from point A to B, and to whom utter stillness appeared to be his default state of being.

But perhaps it wasn't smugness he was attempting to convey, I realised when the creature's voice shook my organs so violently I almost retched them. I might have, if the teeth weren't clenching so hard I started tasting iron. "I can just take whatever I want from you, human," he decreed without leaving a single doubt.

My eyes watered and I swiped at a runny nose... which was of course dripping red snot. Outstanding. "No need to shout, my hearing isn't going just yet. Wasn't, anyway..."

So negotiating a deal was off the table. Figures. How had I dared to expect any different for briefest of moments? At least I scored an irrelevant victory against preachers, who were obviously full of shit on the subject. If only they were here to witness me in my full glory.

"Or is that your aged ears are struggling? I knew this grandma..." my big mouth kept on slurring.

"Why are you still here, human?"

I was here first, asshole. I huffed and went for easy-going instead, "What, was I meant to piss myself and hightail for the hills because you're so spooky? Where do you even see those around here?" In all honesty I probably could have lost control of my bladder, judging by painful clench my other organs did. One point for dehydration.

"You must be one of the dopey kind. But why do you reek of so many aspects of death?"

"Yep, that's what they say about me, dopey and kind. Or kind of doped up? Actually, what did you just..? I think my ears are ringing a little too loud for some reason," I shook my hammering head in an exaggerated grand gesture. I raised up my eyes to stare indignantly at the ancient devil to complete the pantomime but the road was empty. My mouth went slack. So he got sick of my ramblings and left.

... That's fine, I still had all the dead people to keep me company. Perhaps a beast or two will slither in later in the night. Surprising they hadn't come yet. The wait was worst part. The quiet, unchanging stillness. Just me and my thoughts.

A giant shadow crashed in and stuck to the exposed brick wall with no sound at all. It wasn't ground floor. I hadn't screamed in surprise only because I was exhaling.

"Have a thing for dramatic entrances? I can appreciate that," I nodded to relieve some of the tension. Hardly worked in the presence of low growling emitted by an overhanging beast. It was actually hard to breathe. My lizard brain was trying to claw itself out of the bone cage and leave.

He was holding his massive body up by the tips of fingers, clunky boots also only barely touching the crumbling wall by their studs... which, upon closer inspection, were actually two protruding claws? It shouldn't have been surprising sight, especially given the looming crown of bone. Yet it was. Who does that to perfectly fine shoes? Why bother with them at all? But all of him was hidden one way or the other. Hood hung down so low even he himself couldn't have seen anything through it.

He probably hadn't. There was constant noise. Was the disturbing reverberation throughout my bones an echolocation?

"So you're not afraid of me, are you?" Noise screeched inside of my skull which had started to feel hollow. Contents must have all went dripping down the nose. I sniffled it in. He had to have been smugly mocking me this time.

I waved my hand streaked with browning smudges, "What, this? Your deep sex voice just given me most massive boner. Completely normal." Brief brush with silence reminded me of terror of being left alone. "I've seen worse," I said truthfully for once, trying to see into the dark hood.

"I can see that," he agreed out of the blue. I had expected ancient horror to argue.

"Can you? See."

Beast dropped down in a calculated move, avoiding detritus and my limbs - even though the claws were startlingly close.

"I can. I don't want to."

"Huh," I replied dumbly and looked around. I really could have done without seeing most of the things I've seen too. "So you don't see shit."

"Thankfully," he mumbled in agreement and I chuckled. "But I can smell blood, cum, old sweat of many people. Drugs. Mould. Metal. Rotting injuries. All manner of man-made misery."

Of course he didn't need the sight. Nose alone probably has given poor demon a sensory overload. I threw my hands behind the neck and reclined as comfortably as it was possible in this situation, masterfully containing a wince. "What can I say, I know how to party."

"All partied out and ready to die," it was a question but he stated it matter-of-factly. The understanding was oddly comforting.

"Yea, the hangover is killing me," I tried for mirth but it fell flat. Boy was I cold. Swished my hand around in circles with impatience, "So if you could just wrap this up already... Preferably same way you did the girl. That'd be swell."

"No," he all but growled. I gaped, miffed. Obviously I couldn't tell ancient horror how to do his thing. Swallowed.

"Fine."

"Fine what? You really should pay more attention what you're agreeing to."

I scoffed, "As you've already pointed out, my will holds no water. That was a resignation."

"Perfect. A pet who already knows his place."

All my fake amusement fled the body. Chilled limbs which I already barely felt got fresh wave of coolness and it had nothing to do with the timbre of its voice for once. Cold sweat made me shudder. Breathing sped up and I felt lightheaded. I can't do this again.

I lurched past the creature, towards the open space. I wasn't high up, I wasn't able to crawl far before but perhaps if I land just right I could snap my neck. Or bleed out - there couldn't have been all that much remaining.

A clawed sole lightly pressed down on me and it felt like tree had fallen. "Death is not an escape. I can repair the tissue. And I assure you, I can subject you to fates much worse than whatever you have been through so far. Things you've no imagination for."

My inadequate creative juices started flowing anyway. If the flesh was his playdough, he could make me part of himself. I could be made into a sentient appendage. I could be screaming into dark void until something worse came along to change that.

The shuddering grew worse. It can always be worse. Why do I always linger and dare to hope for anything besides that?.

CHAPTER 2

I woke up with a distinct sense of motion and wasn't freezing anymore. Was I in a car? The shadowy scenery was definitely passing by. The seatbelt a tad constricting. I tapped around to get better sense of surroundings. Right. This was definitely not a car. The demon was carrying me, saying nothing. I stared up at the silhouette of horns which were faithfully keeping vigil ahead and firmly ignoring me.

Annoyance overtook me. I proceeded to play drowsy idiot - which I mostly still was and slapped the creature around some more, eventually landing my palm onto what should have been its face, wondering what the ancient horror looked like under that.

Teeth clamped down on my knuckles and I pulled the hand back. Angry red scratches reached all the way to the fingertips and one nail could have been missing. I held back a yowl and slew of curses. The whole of it could have come off clean, had he wished so. Was it worth it? Absolutetly.

I slammed same wounded palm back onto creature's rumbling chest, which he apparently didn't mind, and proclaimed, "You spoil me, good sir! I could get used to traveling like this." I got him bloody. The well-worn scraggly leather beneath my hand was rough and crusty though, so it didn't make me feel any better. It had to be just a drop in sea of what already was caked in on it.

"We can keep your legs permanently broken to make this an ongoing arrangement," after just a moment's thought he said softly, as much as that was possible for something whose entire chest was rumbling to create sound. He did not speak with his mouth.

I made a sour face at the expense of his blindness and almost didn't say it. But ended up nodding, "Mhm. Anything to avoid slogging through this landscape. Carted around like a royalty by a monster, no less. Who else on the entire planet could brag about this?" A lot of dead people, that's who. Hopefully I'd piss him off enough to join the ranks soon.

Creature didn't reply. Whether he was getting annoyed or hungry, there was no indication at all.

So perhaps we both agreed to keep my lower body continuously mangled, but it wasn't getting any worse right now. I didn't even feel much pain because everything went numb from hours of being kept still. Nobody was mentioning the elegant breakdown I've inadvertently displayed. Life was good.

I could have asked where we were going, but didn't really want to know. Meanwhile, nothing bad ever happened in transit. Cocked my head backwards and stared at the night sky. Light pollution was much less of an issue since the grid had failed. Most cities still maintained the power with some effort, but it was costly endeavour. In any case, I was nowhere near those. Started humming while stargazing and began falling asleep again. It's probably been a while since I was carried... if ever?

... Vertigo hit me like a brick. Then again. It took me a while to catch on. The monster was jumping around. Something out there in complete blackness screeched and the steady ticking changed into a constant, reverberating growling. It echoed like there was an empty cave within him. I felt like I'm hanging off a precipice. Fear rose. I wanted to get away from the monster holding me, even if it meant leaping straight into another one. The echoing was insane, impossible, nauseating.

Something in the dark didn't get the clue and lurched at us again. The creature which carried me just leapt away again and trudged along without even tightening hold on his lovable bundle. In fact, never once has he even jostled me to rearrange as though the arms never got tired. One more reason to hate these inhuman blow-ins.

"Ha! You suck!" I shouted at whatever it was following in a deliberate attempt to antagonise it. Perhaps the new creature could eat this one, and save me some heartache. Even I heard it scuttle around. On many many legs. A much longer atrocity.

Scampering thing lurched forward again, immediately to be outpaced by the one on two feet. Angry hissing came from all over the place, tippy tapping noise multiplied too even from up ahead. Shit was getting real and he was walking... right at it? Could he even see where he was going, through all this noise? This was probably going there anyway, but I didn't exactly desire to be carried into some big maw.

I turned away from the blackness back to my associate, "He probably took offence to what you did to the shoes. Those aren't sandals, yo."

There was another flat pause and I was starting to get disappointed my jabs weren't landing anywhere at all. It was far harder to cope when even my out loud thoughts just bounced back to me.

Eventually echoing growling formed into, "I'd grow actual eyes to see that thing wearing shoes."

The air rushed out of me in almost a laugh. Relief. But, yeah. The thought appealed to me as well. If I was going to be killed by an unspeakable abomination, I'd want it to at least wear something ridiculous. Flip-flops and a hat? Make that terrifying.

"Your fashion sense is not to be lauded either," I admonished. "Ragged cloak? Middle Ages ended centuries ago."

"They're making a comeback," the reverberations told me and I frowned. And just whose fault was that?

Without giving me chance to retort, he'd slammed into something instead of leaping away like usual. Hissing was still universally present so it had to happen sooner or later. This was it, then. I put all my brainpower into imagining straw hats on them both.

"Ladies, ladies! No need to fight, there's enough of me for everyone," I bravely yelped, enduring another slam, hiss, gurgling roar, crunching, slurping and something wet dribbling down onto me. It felt irritating on my skin and outright burnt the fresh scratches.

While I wasn't concentrating, it was all over and my cabbie sprinted away from all the noise. I was still rubbing the mystery liquid off my skin onto both mine and his clothes. Mostly his.

"You flatter yourself. There's barely enough of you for an animal," collected grumbling informed me.

"Depends on the animal," I shot back. "There are no bears around or anything. Rest would need a group to finish me in one sitting."

"If there was, perhaps you humans wouldn't be so pathetic now."

Then we'd probably be extinct, but I conceded the point in favour of a more optimistic reality, supplied by the ancient dread.

There was more noise in the dead of night, but just one another thing dared to challenge the porter. That one was resolved much quicker and less eventfully. And I couldn't even tell how. Perhaps they... talked it out? I didn't even get a chance to be a smartass.

I passed out again out of exhaustion at sunrise. Woke up in a drizzle. My parched lips parted and I wished for a downpour. How long will this go on? This was starting to be as uncomfortable and as painful as being left back there. If I don't say anything, perhaps I could die of dehydration? Could check and see whether his claims about revival are true. But if so then I'd have suffered for nothing and I'm all about feeling acceptable right now.

"What do I need to do for water?" expecting the worst I croaked out. I could imagine what human would want, this thing though who knows? Stick my hand in his cakehole again? Because for sure it wouldn't ask for a cake.

"You need to look for it in the bag," creature answered and for the first time I'd noticed a strap over his shoulder.

"Oh," I couldn't help but express a surprise. "Can I get my other hand free?" I asked whilst still basking in the unprecedented generosity of my lord and master.

"Only if you stick that one inside me as well," he replied flatly.

Ah, there it was. My gut churned and lips did an unhappy thing, but I managed a somewhat civil reply, "If you put it that way, how can I resist?"

I didn't really need that much mobility, but how could I back out now? The hold did relax. I rested my chewed up palm on creature's chest and pulled up the other arm. Tingles paralysed my whole shoulder and for a minute or two I just writhed. The tireless monstrosity hadn't said anything, but there had to have been contempt for flesh so weak. Well fuck him, hoped his muscles cramped up from all this walking and carrying too.

When I finally got to getting to the bag, I found that it was pink and sniggered uncontrollably. "You will be stopped by a fashion police at the next intersection," I announced and then my mirth fell away as I realised it must have been the girl's.

Opened and greedily gulped down the first and only thing that caught my eye. There wasn't much, so I didn't gorge all of it at once. Sated, rummaged in the pink bag further. Some thin summer clothes, crackers, a single beat up mystery can, jelly worms which I immediately stuffed into my mouth and made unflattering sounds about. This was first food product in my mouth for at least a week.

"Alright, you can eat me now," I announced after achieving complete happiness and splayed out as much as it was possible.

"Later," the chest hummed. Charming.

"Want one?" I wiggled the wormie right in front of him.

"No," I flung it into the hood right as he said it, somehow managing to forget he wasn't human. It just hit something firm and fell back onto me. Disappointing. I suppose it will take a while to relearn lifetime's worth of ingrained things.

I stared into the shade under the cloth. It was overcast, but still day. I didn't see anything under the hanging fabric. The neck was twined in a cloth so black it looked concave. Did it go up all over the head? How did I get bitten, then?

"I will bite it off this time," a growl told me as though he knew exactly what I was thinking. Could he tell where I was looking? Probably..? The breath was warm moving air and probably audible to somebody like him.

"That's fine. You will either way so let's just get it over with." At least the monster had given me candy for my troubles.

"Later," he reiterated.

"Ugh, don't play with your food. Hooligan!"

But that only made me want to do it even more. Initially feigning a stretch, I gathered momentum for a slap straight into what would have been a shadowy cheek. Something caught my arm. I frowned at it. Then frowned some more, just with confusion. His hands were still gripping me like there was no tomorrow.

It was the grimy coat! The leather was twining around my forearm. And I could not move it whatsoever.

"Are you revoking my spare arm privileges?" I asked terribly frowning. This development was very disappointing.

No answer. No give in the hold either.

"You're being childish," I accused, fully aware of being a hypocrite. But he was supposed to be an adult. However hundreds years old and all that!

Quiet yet again. Need to change approach.

"Oh. My. God. If the clothes are part of you are you streaking?!" I whispered, acting all scandalised. Because thinking about it, it was actually weirder for a creature from another dimension to be wearing fancy-ass biker boots.

"The footwear is real," chest had reverberated defensively because he didn't need to reply anything, and therefore it was incriminating. Or so I chose to see this.

"Wow... and that doesn't make you feel... even more naked?" I was hundred percent genuinely curious and also moments away from breaking into an actual roaring laughter. The thing from beyond had, in fact, a sense of appreciation for fashion. Because there's no way he'd be bothered by stepping onto sharp glass with his poor little clawed footsies.

"The guy insisted on keeping them, so I had to take it," now he was outright explaining himself and I did chortle.

Though I don't suppose this happened in a boutique. I gave in and asked, "Are you sure he meant the boots and not his legs?"

"Doesn't matter. I have both."

For once, the sheer absurdity of the event was not completely doused in cold shower of reality and the bleak company I've been forced to keep. That could - and probably would - be me. Even if not soon then eventually. Detours could be fun!

"Hey, can we go there?" I pointed for a blind man like a complete idiot.

Quiet vibration in the chest changed into louder clicks. "We can," he'd replied without missing a beat. I waited for more but it didn't come.

I gave in, "Will we?"

"Probably not," the frustrating monster told me but I beamed. All I heard was that it wasn't a no.

"What would it take?"

"A decent reason," creature deep-toned.

Just decent? Not even a good one. How generous! I concentrated on list of viable reasons for a stroll in a forest.

... Realistically, there was none. A lot of little bullshit ones, but even I didn't feel like bothering. Drying out my parched throat further by being minor (and likely completely ignored) annoyance gave me little joy.

My restrained arm smacked me on the side of the head. Before I could protest I heard him bellow and pick up pace, "Cover your ears."

Immediately I started to protest, but got cut off by another voice. Couldn't make out what they were saying. They were calling? Looked around and into the brush, which lead further into to the woods.

"Now," his piercing tone made me reach for the ears instinctively. I didn't, fully. Somebody was really calling from out there.

"Ignore," the chest besides me snarled and fell completely still. There was no more reverberation, no sound. At all. The greenery was completely still, and eerily quiet - besides the voice, which was getting clearer each time.

My heart started pumping more blood and the headache picked up again too. Something was off, despite nature looking so serene. The day had started to clear up. The sunny outcrop was completely at odds with a sense of danger pumping through my veins. I had finally done as told and attempted not to hear the voice, but it might have been too late? I heard it on the inside.

I felt something seductive, revolting looming at the edge of my consciousness and trying to push in. Visceral fear made my heart beat so hard it was hard to breathe. But I was good at living with fear. Frankly, sinister voices in my head were least of my problems.

Wiggled my toes to get more blood pumping through the legs. Tingling and the pain allowed me to concentrate on other things. For example, a detailed recollection of how the leg was hurt, and whether it was too late to save it. The smell of dried blood on my sleeves and people who were no longer around. The people who were but shouldn't be. I bit on my loose teeth and tasted fresh metal again. Cold anger tempered the terror.

At some point I felt the almost inaudible growl rolling off me again. Opened eyes to find scenery had changed. It must have been safe. Wiped sweat off my forehead and kept the fingers clutching the hair. Man, everything hurt. Physically. Fished out the bottle and obliterated the remaining water. Didn't have any more energy to rip on the ancient horror, even though him getting spooked was a golden opportunity. Whatever we brushed past must have been whole new calibre of monster. Even to him.

Looked up at the hood with its curling horns. Was this guy even something worth of awe? Some crummy human lookalike. Terrifying.

Yanked my hand to slam it into his so-called face, but the coat tightened so hard around it the bones cracked. Best I could do was twitch my fingers and whimper. Having expended all strength, sagged against the devil's shoulder and relaxed.

CHAPTER 3

Slam.

I jumped awake just as the heavy wooden gate bounced off the walls and smacked back to their resting place, whilst the creature slipped past seamlessly. I heard multiple human voices shouting from all around. I didn't need to be awake for this. Closed my eyes again.

I was deposited on something soft. Body, finally permitted to move freely, did so without asking me. Everything spasmed and tingled with sensation of daggers. I hissed and eventually managed to curl up, as much as that was possible. The broken leg professed a hard no to the affair.

The echoing murmurs betrayed multiple presences in a great hall and it forced me to finally take a look. I was in a church. No pews or an altar, but the colourful windows and columns speckled with cherubs agreed with that assessment.

The grandiose space was refurbished with couches, tables and several cupboards. The leather-draped demon looked less out of place than the plain furniture.

Past him, several people hid behind the stone embellishments, all armed with different kinds of weapons. The guns... weren't aimed, but not lax either.

"We... Priest is..." one of them started stuttering louder.

"He's coming," an authoritative growling cut him off and we were all back to awkward silence again. I stared at them, they mostly watched the horned monster in a cloak. My groggy head could not begin to make sense of the situation. Was I to be a ritual sacrifice? Was there to be a spiritual cleansing?

I struggled to sit. The pain was paralysing, but I made the effort. Standing up would have made for a better picture, but this would have to do. Clenching my teeth, I reached for demon's surprisingly human hand and cleared my throat. "I do," I said way too loudly in a domed building and gave myself a stabbing pain in the skull.

"You do... what? Oh," the people began throwing stares around and shuffling from foot to foot. Demon remained unimpressed. Well, at least common mortals appreciated my effort. Found my fingers tracing patterns absently on the hand I was still holding. Man, this was so irritatingly soft! Before I could ask which hand cream he was using, the massive doors creaked open again. Someone of unimpressive stature stepped in, leaving more bystanders outside.

"How may I serve?" the man whispered and it carried just like sermon.

He didn't much seem like a priest to me. More like a bulked-up battle monk, but even so the attire was wrong. Black vest, ripped up shirt and pants, heavy boots and fingerless gloves as if he was some kind of gangbanger. Upon closer inspection the lot of them looked similar. Interesting choice, as people fending for themselves outside of big cities usually opted for many-pocketed practicality of the military gear.

Wait. Was this where the boots came from? I looked around eagerly but saw no bare feet.

"Make him well," growling rumbled on throughout the tall ceiling.

Man in a shredded fashion statement shuffled closer to have a better look at me. His expression did not inspire confidence and I would have bet he actually wanted to make case about a big city hospital. Instead, he proclaimed, "Understood."

The horned creature turned and left before my brain caught up. The gate slammed with a boom again. My mouth was entirely different entity, however. "Uh... Was I stood up at the altar? And by the way, you guys really should have left it up. It feels like I'm missing a punch line."

The biker dude at the front crossed his arms and gave me squint full of thought. I gave him a wide grin that was all teeth. Alright, most teeth. And perhaps somewhat bloody.

"Yo, what the fuck, man?" rabble at the back wondered. The crowd was coming in and gawking, even those from outside. I was tired.

Gangbanger-in-chief looked at someone and indicated me with a tilt of his head. "Everyone out," his disinterested voice decreed and swarm started reluctantly shuffling backwards. Their noise from outside still reached me, but it was much easier to breathe the freezing air in this holy fortress.

I reclined on the sofa like I owned the place, tossing arms out widely up on the backrest and gave pointed look to the leader priest guy, "Everyone includes you, bigshot."

The man in charge looked at me as if I was nothing, utterly failing to impress me. I stared back just as blankly.

"Don't push it," someone else bristled up instead.

Perhaps I should anyway. There definitely was a small chance I could convince them of something preposterous. I was just deposited on their doorstep by their god or whatever with no clear instructions. But I was so beat up and tired. Mayhaps tomorrow.

Conceded with a shrug as though it was worth a try. I got glared at some more. He wanted answers. Tough shit, because I just wanted a nap.

Last of the three remaining raised a hand in a shy wave, "Hi, I'm Almoner... You don't seem to be bleeding anymore. It would be better if we rinsed you off first. There's a tub we can heat up, if you're up for that much?"

I perked up. Hot water? I'd sell my soul for less! Sleep would wait, "Ohh! Could you? Please!"

"I'll go get it going," said the grumpy mouthy fellow - after being meaningfully glared at - and finally made himself scarce. Whatever made him feel entitled enough to stay? High up in leadership too? Didn't seem the type.

"Thank you! So much!" I shouted after him wholeheartedly with full grin on my face. Warmth! This would be heaven.

Man tasked with the chore looked back over his shoulder and returned the expression, seeming much more willing to do the task. That one can be buttered up, I noted. Most could be, with just a little flattery or politeness, but it was good to remember which could and couldn't be. Some were outright repulsed permanently. I had a suspicion their sour-faced leader was so.

Found the youth called Almoner stare at me open-mouthed. He's snapped out of it and asked, "So, what's your name?"

"Six-pack Sam," I blurted out. The guy's gaze dropped for a second and as he caught himself, grew flustered.

"A... stripper name?" he asked indignantly and forced a roll of my eyes - says a guy with religious motif for a name. Well fine, perhaps not overly ironic then.

"You are about to ask me to undress," I winked.

"Excuse me?" "For medical purposes," I suggested and he got even redder. How old was this wide-shouldered innocence?

Our unwilling supervisor interrupted, "Hurry up, I must know what needs done."

"My leg's busted, but it's already mending and I'm not resetting it." It hurt like a bitch, I wasn't going to let anyone touch it ever again. "Rest are just cuts and bruises."

The two looked sceptical and began giving each other meaningful eyebrows, so I had to intercede, "He only told you to make sure I live, not enable me to run marathons." A bit sad that, but I had put my sprinting days behind me anyhow. My current profession was harder on the knees than thievery.

The man in charge hummed with his eyes narrowing again. If angering a demonic deity was a possibility, I'd be glaring at me too. Or slapping the mysterious being for extra chaos and mayhem, either or. Although not just right now - my arm wasn't turning all the way it should have, so that must be at least fractured also. Parallel cuts on the other one looked putrid. Yeah, perhaps no slapping for a little while.

"In any case... Let's go see how that water's doing," shaggy-haired guy suggested and it seemed like a fair compromise for right now.

The two assisted me with my hobbling scrunched up nosed, but with some effort we'd reached the outdoors. Each hop was jostling all of the skeleton. Pain was making me bleary and I just fell into the water without paying much attention to surroundings. I could tell there was literal bonfire heating up the contraption. It worked and that was all that mattered.

"Holy shit," bulky nurse exclaimed as he helped me to pull the clothes off. Yeah, I was pretty grimy, but not all of it was dirt. Was painfully clear as some of the blotches stubbornly refused to rinse away. "God damn, did he do this to you?"

"Nah," I said fighting off sleep. I'm lying, I wasn't even trying. This was heaven, especially after being in the cold for weeks. I could die here and not even care. These people with their poking though...

"You... sure?"

"Yea."

"So he'd helped you?"

"Debatable," I replied dryly.

"Can you tell us what happened?"

"I'm not confessing no sins to a demon cult!" I shouted lethargically.

Dripping medic shot a glance to the side and murmured, "... Albeit we did end up being somewhat like a cult under heel of what appears to be a literal devil, church is merely a building with thickest walls we bunker in in an emergency."

"Yea, how exactly did that happen?"

"Uh, long story," Almoner threw another brief look towards his danger-radiating supervisor.

"Same, same," I related. Curiosity seemed to abate for now, guy stuck to cleaning the wounds where I couldn't reach. Kicked the fire out after water started getting tad too warm. Priest made few relevant inquiries, and after they decided I wasn't imminently dying right this second, wandered off.

I woke with gentle slapping on my cheek and was forced to climb out of the murky water. Got bundled into a towel and was dragged back into to the church. I don't know how I was upright at all. Bath was so relaxing the little hops should have been impossible.

The room smelled like bleach. And that was where I happily passed out. Frankly surprised it took me this long.

I woke to find myself in a blanket, then passed out some more in warm comfort. Next time I rose was still bleary, but no longer tired. Tried to sit, careful of my leg but didn't jostle it for once. There was a splint attached from the hip all the way below the knee. Something similar on the fractured wrist. Various bandages here and there.

Upon seeing the bucket of water my eyes popped out and I tripped over myself trying to reach it. Then tried again, slower and finally had my fill. I'd probably regret later downing it all at once but I was all about life with no regrets now.

There was stale bread and even a dried sausage. Too bad my teeth wanted to have nothing to do with either of those. At least the stomach wasn't interested either!

After prolonged confrontation with the food I choked it all down anyway.

I ransacked their infirmary. Shelves had mystery bottles, and from drying leaves scattered around I presumed most of those were herbal concoctions. The medicine was a costly affair, even more so in the middle of nowhere. I should expect some animosity because of that. There was a reinforced case, which probably contained remainder of cures from the crumbling civilisation. I chose not to have a crack at it.

Candles, flashlights. All sorts of crap. Blankets, sheets, bandages. Clamps and sharp tools, one of which I'd pocketed. Figuratively, as I was yet to find anything to wear.

Nearby was the pink bag pack, which I pointedly ignored up until this point. I sighed and pulled out the girl's summer clothes. Not the skimpiest I've worn in my life, but that wasn't saying much. I was in no way a hiking person myself, but why would anyone pack these to a trek through a wilderness? I was beyond bemused.

Fiddled about and unclasped the splint. Embracing the ever-familiar pain I'd dressed up in a tank top and short shorts. Perhaps they were just shorts, but not on my build. I was scrawny, but still taller than the teenage girl.

Put the cast back on and hobbled my way across the room. It was easier with furniture and walls holding me up, but still fairly difficult as there was no way I could put any weight on the damned leg. I don't remember the pain being this bad when I ran off... Looks like I made it much worse. Typical. It beat the alternative though! Will probably need to keep pushing myself getting my ass out of this suspicious place, too. Was not looking forward to that. Hopefully that's tomorrow's problem. Perhaps the million sores would dull.

I succumbed on a bench right outdoors, sweat dripping down my nose. It was sunny and peaceful. River gurgled by at the foot of the hill, plantlife gently swayed in the wind. Fenced off garden leered at me invitingly.

"Oh. Uh... You're up," somebody stated the obvious.

I turned my head from the idyllic scenery to be a smartass, but shut up immediately. On the other side were the shower stalls, saunas and what not. And the speaker stood in small scraggly towel alone, looking all delicious. I made a show of staring appreciatively.

"Uh... Lemme get dressed," easily reddening caretaker of mine scurried off into the buildings surrounding church. How young and innocent of him.

When he promptly returned with others in tow and I was on the receiving end of several quirked eyebrows, it was my turn to squirm. My choice of attire left a lot to be desired.

I shook it off. Outstretched my arms, "Be welcomed on my humble bench, fellow cultists. Country bumpkins," I nodded to an especially disgusted-looking fellow.

"If whoever fucked you up didn't teach you to keep ye mouth shut, I will," the bumpkin threatened and took step closer, just to be stopped with small touch from their leader. "Fucking fag," he muttered.

I gasped, "Are you mocking our lord's and saviour's taste in fashion? How dare you!"

"Whacha yappin' 'bout?"

"Obviously, the pink baggie and everything inside is his. Didn't you see it slung over the monster's shoulder?" I insisted.

"No, I just seen you hanging off his shoulder uselessly."

"Well then, consider me belonging to him too and get yo grouchy ass busy elsewhere. Chop chop," I clapped and pointed away.

The angry musclehead was both mollified and ticked off more. "You motherfucker," he'd muttered.

"Upgraded to heterosexuality! Praised be," I mocked looking straight into burning eyes. I didn't need to push it this hard, but boundaries were important to find out. He was sent off with a pointed nod from his master before a vein could burst.

"Do you want to get stabbed?" another onlooker wondered without particular animosity.

"It's okay, you guys will keep me safe," tossed them a wink and turned knowing look towards the stoic group's leader, "Especially you." He had no choice and it was painfully plain. I might get throttled before any of the goons get a chance, but judging by the lack of expression he didn't care about my provocations all that much.

"You go way out of your way to be insufferable, don't you?"

I was about to make a statement how lovable people found me, but was cut off without going on that tangent. Priest stated calmly, "He said to make you well, not keep so."

I waved it off without any worry, "Pft, we all know what he really meant."

"You can be made well in the wet, mouldy dungeon where we keep our dead," man with dead eyes said looking straight at me and I knew that he knew somehow - but I played this game for as long as I lived and betrayed nothing.

Also blond nurse's confused expression made me at ease.

"You dog, you're willing to share them with me? That's really considerate," I beamed with my brightest smile. Because really, who keeps their dead anyway? Poor innocent healer boy was at risk of getting cramps on his face from all these expressions he was tossing around.

Priest nodded dismissively, "I can see why he liked you. But do not presume you are safe. If you do get stabbed, I am putting you down there."

Hmmm... "Does that mean he really can revive people?"

"Yes," expressionless leader admitted firmly, examining me still with unchanging glacial stare.

I was an unbeliever. "Does he just say that or you've seen for yourself?"

He kept on staring and it was starting to disquiet even me. Silence got to blondie first, he'd rubbed back of his neck and pointed to the passionless rock of a man, "He dies pretty freq uently... in defence of the town."

Awkward. Quick, need to ruin it. "No wonder you seem like a walking dead," I said to the lifeless eyes and air got even thicker. "... Which makes my brainless ass safe?" I said self-depreciatingly, in attempt to gloss over it but still felt like a complete asshole. I'd have much deader eyes if sweet release kept being refused. And he was doing something useful for others. "Sorry."

"You're an idiot," peanut gallery commented with clear dislike. Could not blame him.

I swear I saw Priest's eyes slightly crinkle with amusement before going back to flat staring. Agh! So he successfully made me squirm and didn't give a fuck about this.

Since the dead-eyed man won this round, I will need to have another go at him to establish dominance. Question was, is losing an eye really worth it?

"Well, I can't be this hot and smart. It would be unfair to you all," I responded to the insult.

"Anyway, what can you do? As in skills. You've a lot of supplies to pay for," a voice in the crowd demanded.

Oof, this would be a tough one. The skills I use to pave my way through life might not be appreciated in a small (religious?) community.

"Hey, that's a little too soon isn't it? He shouldn't be out of bed at all!" Almoner protested fierily.

"But he is and might as well sit on the watch."

"Oh! I can do that," and after the statement was met with disappointment I added, "I guess I can... patch up clothes?"

"Eh... Cities hold onto their craftsmen too well," the taskmaster grumbled.

"Or they just suck at navigating the great outdoors," I chirped in. They gaped at me and I mumbled glumly, "Can't be good at everything."

"And you don't? At scavenging?" Ahh... They wanted somebody to take on the most hazardous task. But I'd need to go out to leave this place sometime, so might as well.

"This wasn't my first rodeo," I confirmed, being firmly on my second big venture outside. Granted, my current predicament wasn't even caused by monsters. "In any case, have you guys got any crutches in this joint? I don't think I can hobble very far like this."

"I couldn't find them. I'll look around more after my watch," Almoner said.

"Oh! Can I join you?"

He smiled and extended an arm for me to hold onto. Gladly used the excuse to get a hold of the sturdy countryside youth and lean into him. It was almost fun walking three-legged with this good-natured guy. Would have been pure joy if I wasn't sweating from all the effort.

Passing through more people he broke down and asked, "Really though, what's with the clothes?"

"You don't approve?" I faked sadness with pouty lips. "Should I cover up?"

He covered up his face instead and began to fidget. He was genuinely young. "No, I mean... You have a nice body... It's just... Not your size?"

"The only other option in that room was blanket toga, and I don't think wry glances would have been any different if I wore that. Although..." My thoughts drifted into a dramatic roman-emperoresque entrance. Tomorrow? Looked around for leafy branches for a wreath.

The young man exhaled deeply, "The bag... really wasn't yours?"

I grinned to tease, "Did I strike you as a pink purse guy?"

The lips pulled on all the bruises on my face and I regretted it immediately, but Almoner returned wide smile which made it worth it. He squinted at me and looked really close, "Well... I can't really tell. Are you?"

That was fair. I suppose I could come off all sorts of ways, especially on such brief acquaintance. Swayed my head and admitted, "I could make it work. What about you, altar boy, how did you end up in leathers?" Gang couldn't have been his calling. The most others had distinctive vibe of being real hoodlums. This guy wouldn't rob a fly. In fact, he just got robbed and hadn't even noticed it. It was a bunch of several keys. Home and perhaps the medicine safe? I put them back.

We arrived at a newly built brick wall and a woman waved as she passed us while leaving. He released me and went up on a patio which overlooked the perimeter outside. I struggled up holding onto the wall.

From up here I saw dismantled houses, bricks of which were used for the project. It wouldn't stop even a determined human, but I guess that's what armed watch was for. How were they dealing with inhuman onslaught? Some of the monsters were unpredictable in their approach. Like the beckoning thing from the trek. There were beginnings of a forest in the distance and I eyed greenery suspiciously. Could that thing have followed?

Almoner sat down, looking at the same shrubbery in the horizon and hummed, bringing my attention back to the conversation. "Well... The guys showed up when near everybody got taken. Either by river, or the woods. They killed the apparitions. Ended up staying. Been teaching us how to stay alive... And now, if they ever decide to leave, I'd go with."

"Doesn't seem like anyone's going anywhere," I slapped the bricks.

"Yeah. It's an okay place to coop up at."

But he hated it here. The place reminded him of all the people that no longer filled the empty places.

"Soo... he was Priest even before taking up residence in the church?"

"Yeah, uh... They've been in contact with his guardian from way back. Mostly Priest, from what I've gathered. Others flocked around him. Y'no, the kids hanging out in graveyards at night with candles and all that stuff," Almoner implored me to understand with mortification on his face. I did, and this was about to become painfully embarrassing for some of them.

Couldn't hold in a chortle, "Do you know which ones were the edgy goth kids?"

Hm. Would it be embarrassing? They did turn out to be right, in some sense. It was still hard to reconcile the world as it should be to what it actually was. The shift had been gradual. In the city one could barely tell. All shortages can be easily written off to the wars we still fought amongst ourselves, somewhere not terribly far off.

"Envy's one. The guy behind Priest just then."

I racked my memories and something wasn't taking the right shape. "The one with steel pipe on the belt?" Nod. "But he's much older than your leader." Priest hadn't looked that much older than me. The dead eyes did seem like they'd seen every thing... But then again, if I didn't try so hard that's exactly the expression my face would make too.

Shaggy haired blondie pursed his lips and considered if he'd said too much or not enough. Eventually just shrugged, "Well, I told you he doesn't die."

"Right," I said and we both sat staring into the open fields that used to be arable land. The village still worked some of it to an extent. Demons or not, people had to eat something. Meat could go only so far.

"The old folks must have loved all the devil worshipers moving in," I tried for a cheerful jibe, but the kid stiffened some more.

"They were all gone by then," he whispered. "One by one walked into the water, only to show up next day. Just being near them, or the water made the mind cloudy, body - sicker. It was like they took part of you even if you didn't go." Almoner shook his head to escape grim memory, and attempted weak smile, "Sorry. I think you're right. They would have hated the Fingertips of the Devil, even if they weren't affiliated with strange things."

I cleared my throat and said with pretend cheer, "That's old people for you."

There were more things I wanted to ask about location, the people, their demon - but perhaps not of him anymore. This exchange was uncovering still raw wounds on this young person, and he didn't deserve that. I took Almoner's hands and he squeezed it back. Steered the talk towards the city, the things I hated and enjoyed.

CHAPTER 4

It's been over a week since I've been dumped in this remote nook and today I've found out there would be a supply run organised into the nearest city. This would save me a lot of walking. Hobbling, really I was much better, but still on a crutch. However, as nice and peaceful this place seemed, I was on borrowed time. I did not know when the demon would amble back in nor what his nefarious plans for me would be. I wanted nothing to do with best of anyone's unwelcome intentions - and the creature's mere presence froze blood straight in my veins.

After observing which car they were loading with goods to trade it unsurprisingly turned out to be van - I limped in and hid under the stacks. Might have been a mistake. The produce was heavy and the road - long and bumpy.

As they began unloading the sacks, I heard monotonous voice say, "If you want to leave, leave. Nobody was stopping you."

Didn't as much as flinch. This had to be a trick. I was too far back for anyone to have seen me yet. Another heavy bag was hefted out and steps receded into distance. Voices spoke some ways away. I risked glancing out the wide open doors. There were multiple buildings outside.

"I know you're there," heard Priest's dispassionate voice again, right before he showed up from behind the corner to handle another sack without as much as glancing up at me. He didn't care.

Fine. Fuck's sake.

I carefully climbed out and crossed my arms. Should I say anything? Or just shamble away as fast as I could whilst I could?

Another mean looking guy from Priest's posse was supervising unloading with a rifle. City guards took no chances either. As relaxed as Priest appeared, exchange of high valued goods sported a chance to go iffy at any time. Hungry denizens, exiled bandits, militia ordered to appropriate the food for common good you name it, it's happened.

"Take care," utterly disinterested man bid me farewell. I turned towards speaker and a pear flew at my chest. "I'll pass the goodbye to the kid from you," he added to get me moving, but making me feel like crap had the opposite effect.

"Wait," I called out to him and the man stopped, staring at me with those expressionless eyes. I've never gotten a chance to talk to this person again, but this I really burned to know, "Can you die? If you wanted to."

His stare bore into my soul for subjective twenty minutes and an objective several seconds. So I suppose I had no right to ask or know. If I could I would have taken the words back. Priest's lips thinned but eventually he said, "Anything can die."

"Had he..." How does one ask a potential victim of unimaginable suffering if he'd been through it? By now it was easy to assume words the monster had uttered weren't idle threats. Dismissed that inquiry. "Will you be in trouble for letting me go?"

Priest shook his head, "There were no other instructions."

I exhaled pure confusion. At least it sounded like I was never in any supernatural trouble. The otherworldly thing just helped me, out of goodness of his heart. Yeah, unlikely. Great time to bolt.

I shambled closer in while grinning to pat disgruntled person on the side and said, "Well, anyway. Thank you!"

I turned away to check the haul in my fist. A hardcandy and car key. This will not be of use. "Hey, you," I called back and when the detached man looked over his shoulder, I lobbed the key his way and hobbled off as though I stood actual chance of running away. However, odds were in my favour. Nobody wanted altercations under so many hollow eyes of riffles.

Neither my theft nor the abduction of my very much looked for crutch went unmentioned. The immobilising splints couldn't have been cheap either, on top of the medicine. Nothing rotted off, although I was sure some wounds were well on their way there. Perhaps I could obtain some valuables and pass them along later? Clearly devil worshippers come by here to trade every now and then.

I reached the manned gates and had to do long and tedious entry process. Since I didn't possess official papers of any kind,

I rattled off information of one of my affluent clients. Not contact information, god forbid. Just something I've glimpsed in the man's wallet unsupervised. Old databases had collapsed for the most part, electronics couldn't be spared for each little whim. Documentation was iffy at best.

I should have just looked for holes in the decrepit buildings at the perimeter further out to avoid all this hassle, but didn't want to strain my barely able body. The process considerably shortened after I'd noticed clerk eyeing the pear, which I'd relinquished into the care of state.

I wasn't entirely surprised to find myself in same city I started out at. It was the biggest hub in the region and there was definitely safety in numbers. Small towns disappeared off the map at an alarming rate, whilst big ones remained. Population in those boomed due to orders of mandatory evacuation. However, coercion ended up being unnecessary. Most people voluntarily abandoned their livelihood for shabby shelter away from the newly untamed wilderness.

Double amount of people crammed into same or even smaller plot of land, as the lavish suburbs have suffered the fate of the surrounding villages and ended up on the other side of the fence. Buildings grew taller to accommodate everyone, not that everyone was lucky enough to get a room. There were slums, surrounding the bastion of civilisation on all sides. Nobody who had a choice wanted to be anywhere near the outer wall. In other words, home sweet home.

It took a fair bit of effort and time to reach familiar neighbourhood. Sun was already setting and I was thirsty, hungry and exhausted. So, the usual.

Pushed on the peeling blue door and hobbled in. The stillness told me the most others were already out working, legally or otherwise, so I turned for the stairs towards my room. Hobbling up those final steps left me quivering and completely wiped out. Knowing finish line was so close made me feel all the hurts anew and at maximum intensity. Opened my room's door to find... a bare mattress. I sighed, and fell face first into it anyway. Rest now, find out later. At least it still had this much.

The later didn't want to wait, "Who keeps leaving the doors open? Were you born on the bus?"

I replied without energy to move, "I might have?" It was an ongoing joke among us, most of whom were orphans. Glad some things didn't change, even if buses were a thing of past.

"Oh. My. God. Ruby!" a girl shouted with all her might and I swear flakes fell off the ceiling. "Ruby hurry up and get your ass in here! Now!"

The happy hops soon landed on the mattress besides me and I could not contain joy, either. Sure, jostling hurt but that was some distant and irrelevant sensation. Clasped my dear friend and saw tears rolling down her face, too. Finally, I was home. Squeezed her to me tighter.

"Where have you been, we worried so much!" the ball of energy kept clamouring too loud.

"So much you threw out all my stuff?" I grouched. "Rude."

Even more impudently, knife bearing man barged into the room just to stop and stand perfectly still. Right until he slumped backwards into a jamb as though legs gave up on being there and offering support.

Amber paid no attention to the convoluted process of fainting, all her attention was concentrated on injustice I've suffered. Her nose crinkled as she shared the gossip, "That's Peach, you know how jealous of you she is."

"Oh, that bitch!"

"I know, right!" Amber was as outraged as me as we delved deeper into the blather.

Red-haired man finally regained use of his extremities and fell into a hug, too. Sans the knife, I was happy to notice.

Redhead muttered, "I have some of it, but I didn't know what was yours. We will get all the rest later."

We giggled and caught up a little more until Ruby's dimpled cheeks lost their lustre all of a sudden, leaving a screaming letter R to stand out all alone and angry. It ruined his pretty face, but that wasn't the worst of it. The meaning, the reason behind it always made me angry. About as much as he'd seemed to be now. Without any trace of previous mirth and full of intent to force the answer if he had to, knife wielding man demanded, "What happened?"

I sighed and forced an embarrassed blush and averted the eyes, "I got lost."

"River," Ruby insisted.

"You know the farm with all those tasty zucchini patches? Yumm. So anyway, they're reaaally overgrown this time of year. And the corn..."

"Rivis."

"Drop it," I said in a serious tone too. I couldn't withstand his burning insistence, not for long anyway. I hoped my best friend would read between the lines too.

"Who did this to you?" he asked calmly, clutching the handle of the hidden knife behind his back.

This would not be dropped.

He did know everything else. And I knew everything there was to know about him. The good, the bad, the ugly, the absolutely atrocious. I didn't want him to get hurt. This guy had no self-preservation. And no sense.

Redhead's steely eyes were unblinkingly fixed onto mine. The discomfort was caustic, even though it should be like second nature to me by now. Mostly because I knew the intensity would not diminish for days and days I've tried vexing him with silence before. After all I've been through this should feel more like a mother's embrace. It didn't. I was far too tired to do this dance now.

"You've said the bald guy with rings was bad news," I whispered, looking at the putrid floorboards.

"You didn't!" Amber's light brown eyes gaped in surprise and Ruby's turned into a scowl. He knew the man first-hand. My best friend attracted bad apples like an ever-growing pile of rot. And I knew for a fact it was on purpose. It wasn't his fault or choice, but he used it to the fullest to let the rest of us dodge that bullet whenever possible. I didn't approve.

I rubbed my face and sighed again, "I didn't but he was there... And frankly I should have known it would be nothing good as soon as they said it's out of town." But it was good money. Would have been. We had mouths to feed.

The two glanced at each other and I read them like bad news in the forecast. "Cherry and Lime went with some people to party out of town," my plumper friend offered.

Dread was chilling me from the inside and I started shuddering. With memories, with foreboding. I gripped Amber's hand and her nails were digging in too. They saw what that place did to me, the bruises were still green and yellow all over. We all had run-ins with bad clients. They knew I shouldn't be here, alive and telling tales, especially after so long.

We all felt it. Our friends weren't coming back. And there was nothing we could do. Militia wouldn't leave the city to look for some dead hookers. They barely cared when one turned up in the middle of street. And it was pointless to go on our own, even if we could. Which we couldn't. I didn't even know where it was.

I grabbed Ruby by the shoulders in my powerlessness, "Why? Why would anyone go there after me?"

"We didn't know," he muttered through his teeth and my powerlessness crystallised into something entirely different. "Peachy didn't tell you. Of course. And why did I think to trust her. No wonder she was so quick to..." I was prattled on, frantic and enraged. Then fell quiet but my thoughts still swirled.

Fuck!

My desperate anger was completely dwarfed by the immeasurable fury which started brewing within Ruby, replacing all that powerlessness and despair. He looked out for all of us lost souls. He felt responsible, for whatever reason. The R on his cheek might have told everybody he was a rapist truly ironic for somebody in our profession but we'd been through some shady circumstances. He'd earned some kind of brand. And now there was somebody at fault.

I knew he'd kill her. And hell, I would be right there beside him.

No no no no. I let the resentfulness grow for just few breaths more and forced myself to take a step back. Grabbed redhead by the wrist, "Even if she's a stuck up bitch who didn't tell you all where I went, she couldn't have done it on purpose." As therapeutic as this could have been, it was a risk.

"It happened and now two more people are as good as dead," wiry redhead stated so coldly it was clear nobody would change his mind. And what he said was true. We were the only people who looked out for us, and she'd stabbed our little family in the back. Even if it was due to sheer stupidity. He was making a very compelling argument for me to keep spiralling.

"Why would she do it on purpose?" Amber uttered and I grabbed her into my arms. She wasn't a creature capable of anger and I loved her dearly for that. It's what finally doused my embers to stillness. I shouldn't let this go too far, for her. And the other not yet ruined kids. We didn't need more misery in our lives, whatever the kind.

Yet, the answers to her question ran through my mind uninvited. For their things, too? Covering her own ass? Absentmindedness? She knows something we don't? Has a deal with them? It just didn't matter. Neither of us grim ones addressed it.

He must have seen the look on my face and uncharacteristically relented. Perhaps due to the actual look of my face rather than the surrender itself. "I am branding her with a K," redhead stated and I sighed. It was a valid compromise. Peach would be known as killer, and somebody somewhere would end up beating her to death for it. It was an imperfectly perfect solution.

"Amber, would you give us a minute?" I asked.

Ruby tried to make a swift but valid escape, "No, you two stay here. I need to talk to Star's girls about all of this anyway. And then go work."

I made a mean smile pinning him right to the wall, "Perfect! Amber can pass the story along. You sit back down."

"Yeah, leave it to me! You two need to catch up," brimming with desire to be of use she'd jumped up and shouted from the doorway, "It's so good to have you back."

I smiled tiredly and when sound of her energetic steps disappeared, patted the spot beside me. Ruby looked at me with the weight of the world and sat down, turning his gaze away. He was tense. I knew he'd lied. He knew I knew. He also didn't want to bother me with this. But I wasn't going to let him carry the burdens alone. It's not how any of this worked. I bumped his shoulder, familiar gesture meaning I'm always there for him. With him. Whatever he'd decide or needed to do. Regardless of my reservations. Whether it was wrong or right. He relaxed considerably, but one of the hands was still hidden from sight.

Ruby's decisions have never steered us wrong. Well, okay, they have but we were alive. And through all of those we'd learned not to give out cheap second chances. Scorned will always harbour ill will. Mercy only invited open wounds. So I knew he'd be removing the problem with the root. I understood it. Just... those decisions didn't come easy to me. And that was why he was the one who carried us forward. He kept houseful of discarded people alive and therefore deserved someone to have his back. No matter what. And I always would. Regardless of everything. Even if Amber would wonder. Even if the kids would miss their caretaker.

Logically I knew this had to be done. Even if the snake was completely unrelated to people at the mansion now, she could still seek them out for whatever vengeful reason. Could alert them that I was back. She'd need to disappear tonight. But why did I feel so shitty? I don't even like the chick... but I still thought of her as family. Hell, it wasn't all bad or we wouldn't have taken her in. Kids loved her and she'd braided hair for everybody. She even nursed me that one time I had fever. Why did it even turn out so sour?

Reoriented myself, remembering what she'd done to Cherry and Lime. They're probably locked up in a cage in that cold damp basement. Hurt. Maybe dead.

"You've been at that man's mercy for a month," Ruby finally spoke after a long silence of us just sitting in the dark. Our thoughts ended up in same exact place, although I knew the paths we took were different. He wasn't trying to psych himself up. He never averted gaze from the deplorable, no matter what it was. He did it so nothing would bother or surprise him. And nothing did anymore.

I sighed and rubbed my face. "He was there for only few days. But the company he keeps... or, kept him was more of the same."

My friend knew first-hand - he had been badly battered in just few hours. Ruby was tense again and I forced his fists unclench to hold my hand.

"It wasn't that bad," I said. "Not all the time. Sometimes they'd just lock us away and forget for days." And that's when the bodies started to drop. Turned out, people needed water. And bandages. And clothes.

"That's not any better," he'd responded and I shrugged, not wanting to argue. I didn't know which way was preferable either. I hated just waiting for anything in general, but add some darkness, cold, hunger, corpses, stillness and expectations of something terrible coming and oh boy was it a treat. "I should have killed him then," my best friend spat out, but that man with all his jewels was bound to be missed.

"Wouldn't have stopped the other assholes from enjoying their debaucheries out in the boonies. And we can't go around murdering everybody we come across," I said brushing his branded cheek with fingertips. K would end up killing him, especially if we stayed near other people. And he wouldn't leave the rest to fend for themselves, nor bring them out beyond fortifications into the danger.

"That reminds me. I wasn't there for the entire time. Escaped few weeks in?" Told him about unlikely assistance from a monster and the village of cultists. Ruby seemed to slightly relax again, listening enraptured.

"If you've managed to get away, perhaps we can sneak in and get the others?"

I shook head sadly, "It's actually well protected against the monsters. Guards, walls, ditches, guns, flamethrowers. They went all in to protect for their slice of paradise."

"Then how..?"

I shrugged, "I talked one of the shyer guests to go out for a stroll for some fresh air and privacy." He was nicer than the rest. Still young, still naïve, genuinely believing prostitute whispering sweet nothings. I'd bludgeoned him with a rock. The gullible scion did a mistake of mercy that Ruby was adamant of not committing now. There was just us or them. No room for half measures. The young dirtbag blurred the line and ended up dead.

Lean man shook his head energetically and choked up speaking, "I'd never been happier for your silver tongue."

He's right, it all could have gone entirely differently. I shook off the grimness with memoirs of raunchy misadventures, "Really? Not even that time..."

He knew exactly where I was headed and shut me up effectively with a full-mouthed kiss. "Not even that time," he said breathily after pulling away and squeezing me so tight it hurt, but I'd said nothing in protest. This felt like I was really back. At some point we fell down onto the bare bedding and just enjoyed the moment, gripping each other.

"How's our finances?" I inquired.

"Uh... A bit wiped after getting kids all the stuff for school, but nobody's starving. Bakery lets Amber take some of the stale bread, for one."

"Bless that man," he had to be a little sweet on her, because even decaying food was being traded away. Didn't change the fact he'd helped us out. And it permitted Amber to have a normal job. All in all, I secretly rooted for something to blossom. "We'll need to... I don't know, bring our meagre business his way more often?"

"Don't worry, I'm taking care of it."

I crooked an eyebrow at him in the dark but he knew exactly what face I was making and rolled his eyes. I didn't see it either, but felt the indignation. "I'm promoting the place with the clients, who do you take me for? One even promised to discuss business of supplying food items."

"Ohh," having witnessed a certain village doing just the supplying in question I got several ideas about the matter as well. Though they traded for gasoline and ammo rather than useless paper. Hm. I'm sure I had to know people involved in that. None specific came to mind right at this time. File thought for another time. "In any case, I might need to dip into my savings if that's okay? If there's any left. I've certain debts to reimburse."

"Yeah. Fuck, take everything that's left and all I earn from now on too to return that debt. You need help with anything?"

I pondered. Stealing from clinics would be hard, even if that was just authorisation stamps... but I used to know a guy who could forge prescriptions. "Does the pharmacy near park still have Chunky Freckles? Then I've got it." It would cost me money the actual price of the drugs, on top of the bribe then also cost of materials - and favours for time to come, but that's nothing out of ordinary. Then I'd just post younger kids to wait for the van and pass everything along. Easy.

I caught Ruby's face with both of my palms, "What do you need help with?" His skin was wet. I rubbed man's cheeks with thumbs. He shook his head, not speaking. He hadn't cried since we were kids because tears never changed anything. I hadn't quite ever managed that level of stoicism.

"I'm sorry," I said. "I'm so sorry." I wanted to tell him this wouldn't ever happen again, but we both knew better. This was our fate. One just wouldn't walk back. He thought this was it and it broke the strongest person I knew. He would have been fine. But I was so glad I clawed my way out of there. It was worth it to hold on, no matter how much I desired to expire on the spot time and time again there.

"I better go," he whispered. "Before she finds out she'd fucked up and gets skittish. You stay here and rest," Ruby stopped me from getting up.

"I'll have you know I'm very handy with this," shook my crutch in the air like a club. It was neither heavy nor was I a brute who could wield it so. Despite his wishes and protests and attempts to stop me I got up and followed the man. It would be two of us or neither.

"You are not putting a foot outside the perimeter," was his absolute demand and I relented. I'd just be in the way if some animal gave chase whist we were dumping the body. Which meant the kill landed on my hands. Not necessarily a rule, but I decided so.

I waited in a distant abandoned house near the exit we used. It was taking a while for Ruby to find the troublesome girl, so I drifted back into the good old times whilst gripping this damned brick. I never had to kill somebody I lived with for years. Girls will miss her. Ask about her. To some she was closest they had to a mother. Fuck, it's not like I wanted to do this either. I will miss her, the snake that she was. Is, for little while longer. Peach is just like a moody little sister who never quite grew out of her teenage caprices.

When did things go this wrong?

I heard them coming. She was talking about something giddily. Ruby's posture was tense and he seemed stern. Which wasn't unusual for him. He was a gloomy kind of guy, but some people paid to love misery. Or kick it in the teeth. Who'd be smiling after that? Besides me, but I was whole other kind of beast and this isn't even an introspection about me.

Peachy wrapped herself around his arm and practically hung off on it, not least bit suspicious of her surroundings. Why would she be? Ruby would kill to protect his own. As I watched them approach however, a realisation wriggled into my mind. She wasn't jealous of my things or the amazing personality. Cherry was mother to what could have been Ruby's child we were all dumb kids who would rather have something to eat than get condoms. So verdict on paternity was a coin toss and they weren't even a couple or anything. Moreover, that was ages ago! And little Anna was now short by one actual mom. Was this why? This?

I lodged the stone into her skull as soon as they reached the doorway. The blank stare watched my dark silhouette and I wondered if she even knew why or who, or whether it was a peaceful passing. Ruby held the deceased woman from behind and closed her eyes carefully.

His calloused hand brushed my cheek to reassure, but there was only frost inside me. Without saying anything as though we've done this every single day, he hoisted the dead body over his shoulder and ran off through the window I'd unbarred before. There were plenty of such unclogged passageways, if one knew where to look.

The night was dark with but a young moon lighting the way. He would be unseen by the sentries, or if noticed nobody would bother way out here.

Somebody started up a bonfire on the plains. Which was bad. Terribly, dreadfully ominous. Not a single human would be sitting out there after dark, camping. Not when there was perfectly fine city shouting distance away. It got worse when the fire started moving. And it was clearly something burning, for it flickered and dimmed and I even scented smoke. Smelled like burnt meat. But not one of this world. It sickened me.

"Whoah," Ruby slammed right into my face from his frantic run back.

"Ow," I rubbed my nose whilst splayed on the floor, momentarily forgetting about depressing reality and horrors from another world. Then I remembered and did frantic waving in that direction. "Did you fucking see that?!" I whisper shouted.

"Sure did. So did sentries, people are about to show. Let's get moving," his wiry strength shoved and rearranged the trash to mask our presence. Corpse couldn't be dumped far enough in this situation, which was even more of a reason to hurry. His bouncy impatience showed he really wanted to throw me over his shoulders and run, but it was impossible with the splint. Small miracles.

"Do not panic, we have all the time in the world. I'll let you carry me piggyback later," I quipped lightly, trying to match my hobbling to the pull of his arm around me. He just hissed in response, never a fan of comedy. "And this is where you say it would be cold day in hell when you'd let me ride you like that," I went on without missing a beat.

He was looking around and over his shoulder, and gave no reaction to me. I rolled my eyes and kept on talking to myself, "And then I'd ask about other ways to ride you, we'd go into nitty gritty, the pricing and book the appointment..." Silence. "Oy, nothing? I'm feeling a bit ignored here."

Redhead turned his dimples towards me and I broke out in a smile too. There were lights in the windows now so I saw his tiredness up close and clearly. Ruby said, "I missed this so much I'm never shushing you again."

"I'm giving you three days tops," which was unfair. He was so stubborn he might as well be the mule himself. But then again, I could get pretty annoying. It was a close bet. Everyone around us will be wishing me gone again for sure.

CHAPTER 5

It's been more than three days and there was no give. I've exhausted my best material, including old classics are we there yet and that's an odd way to start a conversation in the middle of a discussion, striking up serious discourse when he's on the shitter. Demanded all sorts of princely treatment and got it. I was even inconsistent!

Today I have doodled moustache on his harsh face out of frustration and got everyone to compliment the looks. Everybody went along with it without any convincing. So I was cheating neither it was verbal abuse, nor coming from me but I was getting desperate. Call the militia on me. Pretty sure he had noticed something was off upon the first mention, but didn't do a thing about it either. Just flashed his beautiful dimples and moved along.

This was... so boring.

I fell into a chair dramatically, "You all are killing me... What's with all this coddling? Where're all the biting words, my mental stimulation? This is a maltreatment. My fabulous brain will rot away."

"It's like we'd have a new kid... but from a well-off family?" a boy of around twelve, maybe fourteen said. He was as serious as Ruby sometimes. Yes, I was a terrible example for all these kids.

"Isn't he just the cutest," Ruby said, ruffling my black hair. It was about time to cut it, fringe started getting in the way. "Go along with it."

"Listen to the voice of reason," I snapped with no finesse and pointed at the child, who had potential of snapping sooner than Ruby. He was called Dentist for a reason. Didn't cause problems at home and that was all that mattered to us. Perhaps it should. But again we were no parents of the year. More like every other weekend.

"Hmm," Ruby pretended to give it thought, circling his fake moustache with thumb and forefinger and sipped tea.

"I surrender, please stop this," I begged. "I know this is hard on you too, just... let it all out. I need your surliness."

Ruby shook his head, smiling with entire face, "If I knew this is what gets under your skin, I would have done this sooo long ago."

"Youuuu fiend," I hissed.

He was usually so much gloomier than this. It was highly unusual to see him with a twinkle in the eyes. Usually the smile didn't pass the dimples. We lost so much in such short a time, but he was content to have ripped something back out of the life's ruthless maw. I didn't hate it. And it was a sentiment everyone in the house shared. It's why they went along with my pranks, even if grunting and sighing. And I would be sure to use that to full advantage. As soon as an inspiration struck me.

I coughed, straightened up and announced, "So it has come to this. Unfortunately for you, I am three moves ahead and already expected it. I hid your shoes."

The boy who was more of an adult than me muttered, "He is a child."

I saw Ruby's eyes narrow but he huffed and waved the notion away as though I was bluffing, "They're in the rack, saw them."

"What you've seen, good sir, are the shoes that are... left," I dropped the other shoe, proverbially speaking. Ruby exhaled through the nose audibly but was still grinning. Not enough. "Come on, that was a good one!" I cracked again.

"Are my shoes still together?" alarmed, Dentist slid off his chair and scurried into the hallway to check.

An idea. "If you don't get your shit together, I'll start bullying him and neither of us wants to deal with that. Especially me. I can't spare any more teeth, for one," I laid out new terms very seriously and poked the tongue out through the gaps.

Ruby was still grinning. Even more, in fact? "I'll protect you," he promised.

"What about me? I was the one threatened to get bullied," scrawny kid with crinkled bushy eyebrows crabbed, clutching his only pair of footwear by his heart.

"See, life is tough and unfair, kid. Gotto learn that some time," being a benevolent role model I proudly bestowed a life lesson onto the orphan. His lips curled into a scowl. Outstanding, he could really be my replacement Ruby! As long as the child doesn't start throwing punches... which was a real possibility.

"It will bother him the most if you don't do a damnedest thing," our red haired patriarch suggested unhelpfully. Mature child glared down at me and nodded.

"Ugh! You're ruining everything," I muttered and regrouped immediately. "But not all is lost. We shall witness whether the pupil can match the master," I intoned deeply towards both of them and the child just left without even rolling his eyes.

"Hey wait!" I shouted after him with a serious intonation and sullen expression popped back out. "So, how would you like to have a new friend? I swear, I'm very immature twenty something year old, we'll get along great."

Dentist sounded unimpressed, "That's what a pedo would say."

"Just look what he's offering me! Ruby, reconsider, or you're soon gonna be replaced," I gestured to the empty doorway with great enthusiasm.

Nothing. All I got was a peaceful smile as he gripped that damned hot water in his both hands. He probably saw something unpleasant on my face because finally offered a lifeline and egged me on, "We've got a lot of obnoxiousness to make up for. At least a month's worth. Chop chop."

I tried to muster up enthusiasm, but my fire sizzled and extinguished again. Stood up and paced in front of perching friend. I was not above begging, but tried dressing it up in a jolly tone, "I feel like I've returned to a wrong house. Why's everyone so nice to me? After a life we've led, that is highly unusual, yano? I feel like I'm about to die. Am I?! Do you know something I don't? In fact, who even are you and what have you done with my best friend?! And wipe off that awful doodle, I can't take you seriously."

"I'll take everything you give me with a smile and won't ever take you for granted again," his low tone promised with conviction, eyes burning with intent and I just...

"Ugh," corner of my lip curled in disgust. "Look, I'm turning into you now. Do something about this."

Ruby grabbed onto my wrist and squeezed so much it hurt, trying to convey something words just could not.

"Ugh, stop," I grouched but soon gave up struggling. All my pretend high-spirits evaporated. Wrapped my other arm around his neck. "Fuck's sake, Rubine... Please go back to being normal. You're my solid ground. When you're freaking out... You're making me very afraid. And all this indulgence... makes me feel fragile. I just can't... feel... like I'm breaking. Not here. Don't do this to me."

I had to make everything a joke. But when nobody was laughing, it wasn't a joke anymore and I had to face all of the serious things.

"Okay," he exhaled into my neck after a while.

I peeled him off me and saw the emeralds brim with yet unspilled emotion again. Fuck. I'd never realised how close to breaking point this man was. Always so collected, just rolling with the punches. Rolling them out, to be more precise. I'd never seen him like this. Because we'd never been forced apart like this.

"Everything's okay," I said. Would things ever be okay anymore? This little field trip seemed to have shattered the ruby inside of him... I'd hate to even consider how mad I would have gone if he was the one taken. I barely had the willpower to keep myself alive, much less to deal with others' crap.

"I'm okay," my best friend whispered back after containing maelstrom that was on the verge of breaking out. "Now, where the fuck did you put my boots?"

Clinging to pretend-normalcy I cracked a tentative half-smile and feigned confusion.

"I have to go pick up rest of the supplies for your new buddies," Ruby added as if it was my business, even though nobody asked him to meddle. But the man gave me an honest to god glower so I didn't mention such irrelevant details.

"Oh, you'd love them. They're all scowl and murder, too."

"Boots," he insisted single-mindedly without letting me launch a distraction.

"Hm? Did you misplace them?" I asked in a baby talk. Before I could suffer ire, I attempted an escape veiled in an actual helpful manoeuvre, "Tsk, tsk, tsk. Let's go look for your lost footsie covers."

"Riverrr," he'd grabbed my retreating form and tickled. I squealed, shook, elbowed him in the face and eventually capitulated right after slamming my knee into a corner of something or another. Now I couldn't walk on both legs.

Alarm in his wide eyes was obvious, but we both ignored it. He went to retrieve the footwear after depositing me on the couch and I immediately limped out of the house with manic glee. Ruby would not be thrilled to find high heels there.

CHAPTER 6

Life was back on track. I could almost walk without support if it was just from room to room. Perhaps the thigh wasn't hurt as badly as I thought. I even resumed working in a limited capacity. Didn't entirely need to go all out, as Ruby had completely hijacked my project of returning the favour. I left him to it, it was a losing battle to argue with the stubborn bastard.

I lounged with the other freeloading homebodies in the downstairs den, occasionally assisting the kids with homework as the oldest and wisest in the room. Spouting nonsense about which I had little to no clue was just one of the perks of adulthood. Foolish youngsters! They'd soon learn they were the only ones they could rely on.

Dentist gave me a stink eye and called out to his peers, "Can't you see he's dumb as brick?"

This little shit!

"Not smart enough to help, but just enough to criticise?" I threw back at petulant child. He was well on his way to a wiser adulthood, and all thanks to me.

The boy sullenly sagged into himself and piped down, looking his age for once. I sighed and rubbed my face, "The wiseass is right, go get an actual adult. I'm just here to look pretty."

Dentist looked at me with suspicion as though expecting to get kicked and when that didn't come, turned and thundered up the stairs to the bedrooms.

A rowdy girl named Dancer plopped on my lap and I felt the bone shatter under her weight all over again. She haven't noticed in the slightest, hopping up and down and saying, "I liked your answer better. I'm telling that to the teacher."

"That's a bit pre-emptive? We haven't heard any other alternatives yet. Perhaps you'll prefer... like, the real one?" I ground out, shifting her onto the healthy leg.

"Nu-uh! Your answers are the best! They make everyone happy!"

"Well, if you keep that up, you'll end up being a comedian like me and mean people like Dentist won't like you anymore," I said hearing people descending. Couldn't let the little brat get complacent. "Then I won't like him first!" she threw her wild curls over the shoulder in a manner I could only applaud... Perhaps I could adopt this one.

"What?!" the boy ran down last few steps and was frowning unpleasantly at me again. "I wouldn't ever not like you!"

"Uhhhhh," I hollered and the gang of little ones joined in.

"Children, children. What did you all need help with?" Amber was roused from napping, if those mattress marks was of any indication. Expression still weary after her day job, but tone - willing and enthusiastic. Perhaps this was why the shop really kept her.

All the others must be out. Even brats knew better than disturb the rest of earners.

Rowdy gang settled down and listened. I was so enraptured with the truth I started snoring. I knew for a fact I'd slept because I woke to an empty room. There was banging and shouting somewhere close by. Groggy mind couldn't work out the details but panic roused me into full alertness. I was drenched in cold sweat and didn't know why.

Pitched voices of girls and barking of several men out in the foyer. That voice. Voices. I knew exactly what that was about without really hearing them. They started looking for more playthings but nobody was game.

The speech came into focus, "... You whores dare to blacklist us? Us?"

"Slandering to whole god damn city?"

Amber was there, speaking soothingly. I heard the older foundlings too. Little ones knew to stay out of sight the scene wasn't entirely unusual. However, this outrage didn't feel like it would be stopped with words. There would be blood. Moreover, it sounded like since the gig was up, they'd be taking someone with them regardless of willingness.

My powerlessness rooted me to the ground as my family was smacked around. I was frozen to the spot, unable to take a step. What can I even do, a cripple? I was never brawler to begin with. I was a silver-tongued thief. Shall I stab them from behind? No, no... I can't even walk right now, much less sneak.

Shaking hands unclasped the braces lest they get in the way. After all, I ran with leg busted much worse than this. The heavy objects we stashed around the house wouldn't be of use in this situation. I pulled a knife out of the cushion and held it in my sleeve.

I strode out into the danger zone with an inviting smile, "Boys, what's the ruckus about? Come on in, let's sort it out over some tea."

The scene was a complete wipe-out. Two teens lay splayed out on the floor, no visible blood. Another wept holding her face. Amber was in a chokehold and turning purple. Two more kids on the stairs, paralysed with fear but otherwise unharmed. So far so good.

I had to stall. Maybe others will hear of the commotion and return. Maybe Ruby would make it back in time? It was three men, but they didn't grow up fighting other feral creatures for a bite to eat.

"You!" a bearded thug shouted. "Oh man, Mister Nikolas will be absolutely delighted to see you again."

Crap. I was sort of banking on them not remembering me. What gives? You'd think a self-respecting debaucherous scum wouldn't recall how an interchangeable toy looked like.

"Oh, right! You guys owe me a loooot of money, don't you? Did you come by to return your debts? You are henceforth even more welcome. Please, come in," I gestured to the living room. What I'd do with them there I had no idea. But I was good at improvising.

"He'd been missing your smart mouth," the beard informed me and I shuddered, failing to tap into years of previous experiences. "If you know what I mean."

"He'd killed that what's his name. The mister won't even get to see him," underdressed fellow spoke with a leer.

"We can keep him a secret until we leave. I think this one is bound for the long haul. Aren't you?" many-ringed fingers patted me on the cheek almost affectionately. I didn't flinch, but felt sick. And frozen with fear. And panicking, and words weren't coming out, not that they seemed to work here at all. Managed to force out a faint smile.

"Let's take these two and go, would be enough for now," one closest to me concluded.

Oh no no no no no...

"Please, why would you even need her when you've me," I did my money earning lean on the wall. They'd exchanged glances. I pressed on, "The woman cleans toilets for a living, for fuck's sake. Why do you think she's even here at this hour? Completely useless for the job."

I casually brushed lint off my bedraggled sleeve. Amber, puffy with tears and suffocation really didn't look overly inviting right this second. The intruders seemed to be willing to be convinced.

"What about that one?" An expensive-looking shoe turned over the knocked out girl and my stomach squeezed with desire to expel contents again. No no no no no no. What can I say now? Not like people like them cared about young age. In fact, they probably preferred it. Fuck!

"Hmmm," sweaty piece of shit considered, kneeling down. The other lifeless figure was Dentist's. Fool child, it was ten years too early for you to pull a Ruby.

"Look, they're all crap at the job. The working girls are working," I said as nonchalantly as I could and it was frankly an outstanding performance. I even stopped shuddering. Lives were on the line, and this was what I've done best.

"Dumb bitch. Not everybody wants a man's ass," man drowning in the shorts and t-shirt shouted at me with disgust and loathing. Ironic, as the sentiment never stopped him. He tossed the unconscious girl over his shoulder.

Many-ringed fingers grabbed me by the elbow and dragged after him too.

"Wait wait wait," I dug my heels in, stalling the procession further. This probably wouldn't have worked with the waterfall man, but the rings seemed to harbour delusions of amicableness and I leaned on it heavily. "You all haven't paid a dime for the last time!"

"What the hell are you talking about?" the bearded guy frowned, but violence wasn't in the air anymore. Their plans were finally back on the track and situation crossed over into all too familiar territory of business transaction.

"No money - no honey!" I shouted indignantly and the thugs exchanged looks. It would be easier on them if the dumb whore cooperated and went willingly, after all. Sweaty guy groaned and from the stream of expletives I understood he advocated for brutality.

Bejewelled man also groaned, but reached for his wallet, "Jesus! Just give him the cash, he'd done good job. And will again won't you sweet cheeks?" He threw a wad of money back into the hallway of terrified faces and twined an arm around my waist. "I'll even let your friends hold onto it."

"Sure," I smiled wide. How kind. Since we both knew I wouldn't be around to spend it.

Beard fussed within his own wads and threw some denominations as well. They started moving again and my brain was fresh out of ideas. Even bad ones. Feigning heart attack would just land me with legs dangling in the air just like the girl in front of me. I would not be able to escape again. It was time for final stand.

Shuffled the knife down into firm stabbing grip and raised the hand to strike. Upon turning, my lame leg gave out and instead of fatal injury it just brushed through the surface. Blood was everywhere, but it was merely the skin.

Many-ringed man screamed out in pain, but wasn't entirely unfamiliar with survival. He ripped the weapon out of my grip even before I fell, then kneed me in the head.

"You fucking slut! You tried to kill me!"

Another kick into the stomach. He sounded almost hurt. Boo hoo.

Somebody was laughing his ass off nearby - must have been salty waterfalls. "Whachu expect, moron? You knew he'd killed that other guy."

"I guess I forgot! Public service announcement is in order," I got straddled and blade flashed right in front of my eyes. I whimpered and shut them closed as though that would have helped. Knees pressed down on my arms, and jaw in a golden grip. Searing pain made me scream and I didn't immediately realise what happened only when warm liquid dripped down my ear.

"There, that should do it temporarily, you danger vixen. Don't worry, I prefer feisty ones," ornate fingers slapped my face again in a playful manner and I almost passed out. There was a breeze in my mouth. He'd cut my cheek open.

"What..." my dazed mind wasn't catching up quickly enough.

He smiled cruelly, "We will brand it properly later." Ah. I suppose I've gotten a letter. Looks like I wouldn't be able to stay in the city anymore anyhow.

Angry stomping of feet thundered in. A distinct noise of a bone crack. Before I knew it, the scene around me erupted into a brawl. Weight lifted off me and dabber man joined fighting with the knife in hand too, chasing red tuft of hair around.

He's laid out two, but the third must have remembered he wasn't a common hoodlum by then. Thug pulled out a gun. I screamed and threw my uncooperative body on the hand wielding it and then it was all quiet.

Couldn't really tell what happened in that brief span of seconds even if my life depended on it. There was no memory of it. I just saw my best friend in a puddle of red, someone crying over him and the thugs retreating. The still unconscious girl was left behind, as one of them seemed to be too concussed to manage on his own. I struggled to get free too but for naught. He'd protected her at least her, but at what cost?.

CHAPTER 7

Woke up to a sensation of being in a car again. Engine was on, scenery was changing, seat leathery and I wasn't cold. Did I fall asleep on the job? Unusual. There were few clients who even wanted to look at me after the deal was concluded, much less allow a sleep over. And I wasn't one to relax around strangers like that either. There was a nice older guy who'd paid me just to have someone else in the bed at night, but I did not slumber then either. Wonder what befell the man? Haven't seen him in what felt ages... and then I remembered why.

My hands clutched something that could have been a rich man's idea of a decorative blanket for how terrible it was, but shoulders felt chilled so I pulled on it until was sat in a bundle. My open eyes weren't seeing anything, even though sun was out and blasting in full force.

Being dead sucked. And I was expecting more darkness.

I licked dry lips and first time in ages tongue didn't snag onto all the empty spaces. Weird.

Little by little I started poking all other hurts I thought I suffered. I could breathe. The cheek didn't have orifice. Eye - no longer swollen. Arms were no longer charred stumps... but still tied together. Afterlife truly sucked.

Why the fuck was I still with consciousness, able to think these thoughts? I just wanted peace. I wanted not to consider existence without them anymore. Cherry was there from the start, the puny ginger who shared a pitiful-looking sandwich with two boys who'd been about to rob her. Lime was a reckless daredevil who'd join me on stupid escapades Ruby never wanted a part of. And Ruby... God.

I buried face in my palms and tried to scrub away things I was seeing. It didn't work, never did. The nails sunk in and I dragged them down. Sensation made me shudder. Not from the pain, but sheer recollection of having scratched at warm meat very recently.

So I wasn't dead. And that sucked even more.

Now I wanted to scream, wail, punch walls. Powerlessness kept me still. Crying never solved anything anyway. Nobody cared. Not anymore.

I guess I needed to bide my time as I always have - until opportunity presents itself, which it usually did. Perhaps another monster will eat this one, or me. I had to make sure to get absolutely decimated in that case, because apparently this lumbering thing wasn't lying and could in fact put dead and dying flesh back together. Nothing hurt at all. Not even the aches I carried from early childhood.

Its motivation was laughably clear. Just like the pompous bastards at the villa, he had the power and exerted it. Saw what he liked and took it without asking. Seems like dynamics of power wasn't just a human inclination but rather a universal truth. How... eye-opening. It explained how the creature found common ground with those people. They were all the same.

Hey, perhaps it'll drop me dead just in the middle of the road one fine day like that girl? Hell, maybe today was even the day. But who was I kidding? I was never that lucky.

Stared into the blackness of low hanging hoodie. I needed to locate the boundaries. Establish some trust I could take advantage of.

"Unhook my arms," I demanded flatly, raising them in front of me. This time it carried me with one arm only, the show-off. The other one remained fixed at creature's side, not assisting with the quick gait in the slightest. Did the demon not figure out how to walk efficiently yet?

"Why bother? Just stick both of them in," a growling boomed.

"That ship has sailed. No longer interested," I replied frowning, having not a slightest doubt the creature would shear them off clean this time. Seemed fairly serious about that before already.

Whether I was believed or not, the other very human arm went up and unclasped the hooks one by one. I kept raising my arms higher so the devil could reach further and they came very close to the coiling majestic crown. Just as the last clip released I took hold of a horn firmly.

The demon stumbled. Huh, interesting.

Ran the fingers through the tender bone, which was... much more jagged than it even appeared. Grooves within furrows.

I was baffled to find it soft to the touch. I gripped firmer, pulled on the faux bone and creature veered to the side. Growl threatened, but that seemed like future me's problem. I yanked to the other side and creature stumbled again as though ground stopped being firm. Very interesting.

The free arm of the inhuman monster gripped both of my forearms and pressed lightly. An almost inaudible crack. All four bones shattered like a crispy desert, spilling strawberry jam. My grip was non-existent anymore. Fingers twitched whichever way the deformed muscles contracted them due to all the misfiring nerves. My silent whimper became a scream. God damn you, dildo of consequences...

"My, what big ears you have," I gasped out through the physical agony, visual revulsion and the mental horror.

Growl ticked louder, as though with irritation. I grimaced. Oh boohoo, poor him.

The monster's iron clutch relaxed and my flesh followed his. Something moved within and new waves of pain surged as though there were several blades inside, all twisting. It all regained shape momentarily and monster's human hand slid downwards to its position of useless hanging at the side.

I could suddenly place that disgusting crawling sensation wherever I was touched in passing. Writhing, like that awful carpet... which I suppose was only obvious.

I shoved at the massive chest and struggled. The arm which held me up didn't budge. I grumbled and leaned away, using my weight to wriggle out of the grip. Dangling ridiculously I demanded freedom.

"I can walk myself!" I argued.

Otherworldly creature dropped me like a sack of trash and stepped over without slowing.

Ow. Ugh. Ow. I turned over on the stomach and groaned my displeasure for everybody to hear. Nobody cared, as usual. The demon walked on without me. Huh?

Oh. I guess I was free to go and off myself in peace. I smirked humourlessly as though it would be that simple. Limited roaming range? And it was prime time to test the assumption. Jumped up and took two entire steps the other way. Noise disproportionate to the receding figure thundered down the valley and raised hair on my back, "Did I affix your legs backwards?"

I smiled but there was no enjoyment behind the expression.

Would my knees crack, bend themselves the other way and march me back if I didn't stop? It was probably best to spread out all the blatant disobedience throughout the day. I feel it would be difficult to come back from being turned into a flesh marionette. And then I wouldn't have the ability to plunge my face into a ravenous maw.

I was dragging my feet but somehow ended up catching up anyway.

"I'm tired," I complained after what must have been hours. My bare feet were cut up and I wanted to drink. And sleep. And never wake up.

"You are not," low tones rolled off the monster.

I glared and argued, "Yes, I am."

"No," creature ticked silently and I opened my mouth to be mean when more low reverberations came, "I repaired you again."

Mouth remained open. Indignation and confusion were bursting out of me but I just couldn't find right words. An appropriate what seemed to be covered. It was just as the monster had said upon introspection, I no longer felt physical exhaustion. Was refreshed, actually. Wide awake. My legs weren't hurting.

Outstanding - I was participating in a forced, ceaseless march and hadn't even realised it. I suppose monster didn't mind carrying me, but I had to go and make things worse for myself. I mean, nothing new there.

"I'm tired of walking," my gaping maw eventually spat out and I turned towards a scenic looking smattering of young trees and fell flat under one. Leaves rustled in the wind and sun played on my closed lids. But all I heard were chains rattling and saw blade flashing near my eyes. My hands gripped the face, trying to protect myself from imaginary weapons. The grooves I carved out previously were mysteriously gone along with all my other minor ailments. For shame.

I curled into the blanket that I still carried over my shoulders. Jerked, shuddering again before I even understood why. Then threw it off me whilst containing a scream within me for the thing moved. Why can't nothing be normal?

"You seem to have misplaced part of your... something," I forced out politely, looking for a way to laugh this off instead of screeching like a complete madman. Which I wanted to do very badly. I wanted to force alien creature to explain why there was living flap of skin on top of me, and where did he get off walking around draped in the same thing too. What the fuck was up with that writhing carpet?! Why did it undulate so repulsively and...

"You ripped it off me yourself," creature informed me calmly and cut off the torrent of my thoughts as though with a knife.

"Oh... Pardon me," I stammered out. Horned (big eared?) monster stood still like a statue where I'd left it.

"No worries. My body parts are your body parts."

Charming. I couldn't tell whether this was a fact or a weak attempt at a joke. It had makings of one. And he did give me brand new teeth. Or were they gently used? Who's to say? Him. But I certainly wasn't going to ask and find out.

"Hey, I'm not thirsty anymore. Did you do something about that too?"

"Yes."

"So is it like... I'm just not feeling thirsty anymore, or did you somehow make me drink?"

"I infused your bloodstream," monster explained.

"Handy!" I spoke up with way too much enthusiasm. It was interesting information in general, but I just wasn't feeling it and tried to fake it 'til I made it. I wasn't hungry either and guessed something of the sort befell that front too. Did not know what kind of pre-digested meat biscuits it had put inside of me and had no desire to find out.

"Can you make me blond?" I asked with the energy of small child.

"Yes."

I went down the list of utter nonsense just to keep talking. Extra fingers, eyes at the back of my head, gills, tail, claws in weird places. Whatever.

I fell quiet for a moment and monster asked, "Is that all?"

"What do you mean?" my eyes narrowed with suspicion.

"Is there anything else you want?"

Laughter escaped, "You want to make me into a literal monster?"

"Those are your specifications," creature stated.

"No, no. It was all hypothetical. And I get it, you're so cool you can make anything happen," as long as it involves copious amounts of gore. "No need to prove anything to lil ol' me."

"So you don't want any of that?" Was there a disappointment in that damned growl? Need to flex was strong in this one.

"Nnno," I said and fell into disquiet. I wanted other things. To be happy. To have my family safe. To not have been so powerless. All of those things were moot now. I needed nothing. I needed to be dead. And this thing was determined to keep me around in good health for his own entertainment. Entertain yourself away, I'll make it memorable.

"What did Priest get?" I asked with a sugary sweet smile and knew it translated into the tone.

"Everything."

"Um. Was he like... a busty chick before?" I was confused for the guy looked completely average if not for all that facial paralysis thing he had going on.

Tone of the growl changed into something I could call a hum. Was he thinking? "He is my mouth," monster eventually said.

"Are you having a stroke?" I asked seriously but without a trace of concern. That'd be lucky, so no. It couldn't be so.

"It's what that is called. He is part of me."

"A... mouth part?"

Monster nodded as though feeling my gape. It must have been very obvious, even to a blind man. "He eats for me and therefore is able to transform his flesh whichever way to accommodate that."

"So you're... forcing him to... what? Eat other people?"

"He is autonomous," growl barked at me as though insulted. I held in a scoff. Of course. Spoken like a true asshole in power.

"So he eats people voluntarily, I getchu," I gibed further. If the thing was losing patience, it was important enough for me to get to the bottom of broken bones or not.

"He mostly consumes my kind." If you must know was heavily implied.

"You don't get along with your er... species?" I pounced on the titbit of possibly vital information.

There was long pause full of consideration again. Yes, you're talking to a retarded simplify it so even I could understand. I waited, making faces at the blind creature. "There are no species as such," it said eventually. "Most can change themselves to specialise in unique survival strategies."

Fine, I guess it made sense if they all could just grow whichever way they preferred. "So what you meant he eats monsters, in general?"

"Yes," creature scoffed at me, holding back whatever else it would have wanted to say.

"Can he die?" I ventured into a very pressing matter.

There was an expressive pause again. "Everything can die."

Including this horned beast, then. But something else was implied there, for the answer wasn't just yes. "But you won't let him," I half stated, half asked.

Another pause full of consideration and a flame of anger blazed up. Ground my now-healthy teeth, blood and pain free. What understated pleasure. "Why?" I urged on the reply.

"Would you cut your finger off?" monster finally decided on an approach.

"You saw that I would," I countered, teetering on dangerous edge.

Monster's growl was unsettling. Thundering. "There is no him. That is only my body part. His human function ceased the moment I consumed him. He has that form because it is useful to me. Whatever thought he has is only because I allow it."

I grit the teeth. "I'm not a mouth, am I?"

"No," monster growled low. A scoff? Well, utter contempt to you too. Why am I here, then?

"What, I'm not good enough?" Even I didn't know where I was going with that one. It wasn't even teasing. I was slipping somewhere dangerous and couldn't stop myself.

"I don't make lunatics I just met a part of myself. Eternity is a long time to put up with so much whining," monster's reverberations definitely had distaste now.

I cursed myself for losing my cool. How unprofessional. Shouting first thing on my mind would never be a winning strategy, mostly because that would just be wordless screaming. The last thing uttered did calm me at least. Not all was lost. I just need to be insufferable. Easy.

I digested the discontinued conversation sentence by sentence. It made little sense without grander picture, but creature had divulged a lot.

CHAPTER 8

I wondered how long of a break I would be permitted. Night fell and the monster had not moved or said anything. Time must have been a nonconcept to these immortal beings. They didn't even get tired. Or maybe some did? But why would anyone chose to keep that trait?

Several shapes moved along the plains, but nothing bothered us. Could not even see them well. Where was the skull-piercing voice or a many-legged horror? Hadn't called out because I was in no particular hurry to move. And nobody was curious to check up on the booming speech, so perhaps it was safe here.

It got quite cold in my strappy glory with all my junk hanging out. I started regretting throwing away the skin wrap which mysteriously radiated warmth all on its own... Should I go and cling to a leg or something? Still didn't want to break status quo and prompt continuation of the march though.

So I lay down on the grass and looked at the stars. Thickening moon reminded me of last time I'd observed it. Chest panged and I turned on my side. Laying on the cold ground outside reminded of more than just that recent night. My back sought out a source of warmth pressed to it but there was no one. I wiped at my face uselessly, but saltwater did not cease.

The constant, but relaxed ticking had a couple of extra beats and it was immediately noticeable. I did not move, but prepared myself to act. Fucking finally. I heard nothing else, no idea where threat could be coming from. But it was coming for the passive sonar switched to an actual silent growl.

My new master fearlessly awaited. What are the chances something scarier was coming along? Probably low. Though what did I know? Perhaps they just continued existing as a part of another creature and that's what eternity meant over there. Damn, did that mean I'd continue existing like that too if eaten? Ugh. Belated complications. I could ask, but then I'd reveal my intentions.

Out of nowhere the growl switched to a snarl and there were sounds of ripping and thrashing. I still didn't hear any other presence. Nothing at all to give it away. If I hadn't known how rigid the horned creature was, I'd think he just decided to monkey about for a bit. As it stood, this was probably a death match between a mute and blind - a prelude to a joke, one could say, and I regretted this to be a night. I would have been thrilled to see this play out.

It wasn't instantaneously concluded so I picked myself up and started sprinting towards the thicket some ways off. There I could maybe hide or even get eaten? I had no plans after reaching that.

The wind on my face felt great. It's been so long since I dashed at my full speed! These legs saved my thieving ass so many times. I was good at running. And the fool not only healed me, but also given plenty of strength for this.

Sure, darkness made me stumble here and there but thus far I avoided pitfalls. I got an eyeful of the surroundings during the day. The path I chose was as clear as it gets.

As I got closer to the shrubbery, urge to avoid it at all cost rose. It was so overpowering, I stopped without intending to. I couldn't go into there. At all. Something was in the trees, I just knew it. Something so alien a mere presence of it made me want to be away. Leaves rustled even though there was no wind. As much as it seemed I was halfway to fulfilling my plan, I decided I'd die to some other less dreadful thing. Took sharp left… downhill.

I had a sensation of going up whilst running down. The ground was lifting. Damn, falling and going splat would not serve my purpose. There needs to be nothing left. I hit something and fell down on my knees, breathing hard. Scenery had somewhat changed. There was still the brush close by, but plains now had entirely different outline. There was a house, sparse tall trees. Hallucination? Teleportation? One giant landslide? Whatever happened, lucky! Which was suspicious. But then again, I was trying to get eaten so…

The house was abandoned, I saw broken windows as I ran past. After that there were more lone trees. I eventually exhausted my stamina. I was at an excellent condition but it still has been a while since I needed to run for a living. Probably not my best getaway.

There were branches cracking in the distance. Even though it wasn't close, even if I was here for this exact reason, even not knowing if it was actually dangerous… I felt spooked beyond measure.

Mere trees looked so ominous. I began singing as I walked deeper into the darkness. And then I saw the eyes. Just briefly there and gone. My legs locked up and I didn't want to be here anymore. I didn't want to be eaten alive. I hated this place. I wanted to go home.

Pushing away all the things I couldn't attain, I walked into a branch and scratched my face. Complained loudly. Nothing came for me. Sighed nervously and kept walking. Stumbled into tall grass, another step landed me in a puddle. Found silently gurgling stream, it would appear. No mysterious water creature popped out beckoning me to drown, which was frankly disappointing. Sighed and stepped to walk in the middle of it. If I was pursued, maybe this would help me cover the tracks?

It wasn't deep enough to swim, nor was that something I desired to attempt in the pitch darkness. Walked myself back into the reeds on more than one occasion. Slipped. Cut myself on the rocks. Not had a great time, so to say. Nothing ate me, even though I heard movement around.

Climbed out on a lighter stretch when it presented and curled up on the grass. Shivered from extreme cold. Didn't feel my legs again. Damp ground wasn't kind to a naked skin. Why must I still be so miserable? I guess I could just cut myself to bleed out and be done with. I'll do that in the morning once I can look for some broken glass or similar around. Should have taken the jagged rocks with me.

The ancient horror probably wasn't coming anyway. A bit conceited of me to think it would have. But then again, some freaks had way too much free time on their hands and absolutely loved when something didn't go to plan for once in their perfect lives. Hard to say.

I did walk far. Had no clue as to the direction. Probably nowhere near the city. If I stumble upon a road, could maybe find some old signs with helpful arrows. Not that I had reason to ever go back there.

Kept trying to turn my swirling thought vortex away from the great many upsetting things. And the cold helped, forcing me back into the moment. I'd pass out from exhaustion, wake up ten minutes later to shiver. Pass out again. Sun began rising but its rays weren't warming. Eventually the temperature must have risen just enough to keep me under for several hours.

I woke up with a pained groan. Joints were locked up. Was not having a great time. I tried to sit and must have snagged on some branches. Planted my face into the dirt. Outstanding morning. Exactly what I needed to keep desiring to stick around, world. Good job.

To top that off, I felt unmistakable reverberation through the ground. Absolutely outstanding.

"Baby! You've found me!" I exclaimed shrilly in my airheaded girlfriend tone. "I was so terrified." Winced. Was not my best attempt. Sweetness and not sarcasm, dipshit. Playing dumb hurt less than the alternatives. Put your back into it.

Demon hadn't dignified it with a reply.

Patting my side to look for whatever that's managed to catch on the skimpy string, found that it was actually another string. Hooks clasped together. Why was I still wearing this? Made not much of a difference nakedness wise.

Undid the snag they were not much of a problem if it's just an odd one and not whole row. But there was second. And the third, all in weird places. What the hell? My stiff and frozen over body certainly did not flip around so much to warrant all of this tangle. Eyes found the reason for my discomfort who stood still in the shadows, pretending it wasn't here at all.

I grouched out, "Oh, grow up." This tone lacked any sort of pretence. It was too early for this and I was not used to dealing with clients in the morning.

Chewed on my lip in regret. What now? Pain, that's what.

"I thought you're all for causing minor inconvenience," demon's deep rasp rolled down the grass. Creature didn't sound mad.

In fact, this seemed so... "Petty too. What a charmer. You must get all the girls," I scoffed, feeling tentative relief. If the creature equated looking for me with a trivial matter, I was all for that.

What would piss him off? Thus far, only getting handsy garnered a reaction. Which ow I was not a fan of, but was ready to suffer through to know more. What's next on the list? The coat? But if that's creature's skin, irritability would be well founded. I'd punch someone too if they tried to remove mine. Perhaps I'd exhausted that branch of inquiry.

"I get everything I want," demon assured me.

"Wow, such sexy self-confidence. I love it," I hated it, but empty compliments went a long way. And it made my day to make fun of unsuspecting fools. Demon made an extra tick but had not commented.

I was fresh out of things to say and the monster remained indifferent. I was starting to think we probably would spend entire day here doing nothing, just like yesterday. Which left me a lot of time to dwell. Suboptimal.

Boy, was it cold. I was chilled straight down to my bones. I felt them clatter.

"So, what would happen if I got eaten?"

There was a lot of thinking silence but all the creature ended up saying was, "Depends."

Ugh. I groaned. Of course this would be another teeth pulling session. However, demon took mercy on my frayed patience and elaborated, "If you desire specific information, be specific. To divulge even an abbreviated version would take longer than you've left in your lifespan."

Huffed, considering that. I guess I did essentially ask mommy about afterlife just this time it was an ancient demon who actually had the answers. But clearly, I wasn't keen to know individual paths of each of my subatomic particles after they get scattered away from this meat suit... Or was that a subtle threat? Like I wouldn't live to see tomorrow. It was hard to say what went on in that hood of his... if that's where creature's brain was at all. And that's where all our differences stemmed from, I suppose. The alien thing must have struggled to comprehend humans too. I decided to put effort into being more thoughtful.

I tried to specify as requested but realised that I couldn't. It was more or less the same phrase in different words. "If an average monster... bit my face off? Presumably with the rest of the head and or body."

"There is no average," monster rumbled out.

Ugh.

Patience, patience. "What are my options?"

"Your face will be consumed by me," demon's reverberation had more life to it this time. Yes, yes. I was thrilled about this too.

"And if not?"

"Unlikely," the arrogant asshat flexed once again and I rolled my eyes. Sunnovabitch, it's why we're having this entire conversation. Or is he onto me and trying to annoy me into quitting? Oh no buddy, that's not how you win this competition!

"And if that does happen?" I insisted, secretly hoping the creature wasn't as childish as me, for he had far more patience. Several lifespans worth.

"That is a long list," I was informed.

Asking for top three was probably out of question. It was unlikely anybody done polls for monsters' daily gossip magazines. "Start listing," I narrowed my eyes, looking forward to my next pitfall.

"Some just need the minerals and would leave rest of your organic matter in a formless puddle. Others are after entire thing, which they'd use indiscriminately to grow. Certain types just absorb the muscle. Or sinew. Or nerve. Or just brain structure. There are kinds that just take over the body and other humans can't tell the difference. Leeches..."

Yes, we all know about those now, don't we? I glared and cut him off, "So when you eat me I'll become that sort of puppet?"

"No," monster informed me very informatively and I grit my teeth. Patience, patience. Did I really want to know details of that anyway? The bits that I was aware of already weren't promising.

Since being subtle wasn't really going to work here, I just flashed the monster my entire hand, "So, how do I tell apart the things which would decimate chances of my consciousness's continued existence in a nightmarish horror beyond my comprehension after the body's tragically untimely death?"

"You cannot."

I rolled my eyes and wanted to accuse the crafty creature of lying, but sighed and in my infinite forbearance looked back onto the facts. If the monsters changed on a whim, perhaps it was impossible to know.

"Can you tell?"

"Most of the time."

"Ohhh, you've been wrong before?" I took a stab at that infinite pride the devil seemed to be sporting.

"Naturally," he'd responded without missing a beat and providing me with no ammo. How dull.

I guess that leaves burning myself alive, then. In my deep musings I found myself looking at the ceaselessly burbling stream. Still couldn't feet my feet.

"How did you even find me? I even walked through the damn water."

"Was that supposed to mask you somehow?" monster thrummed in a rush as though amused. This grand getaway affair must have looked so pitiful to him that he wasn't even mad. Which stung more than caused despair at this time. "Water spread your smell all over the area. Your feet were cut up too."

Yeah, definitely stinging. Guess the next time I'll know!

Though I was starting to suspect I was in a pit too deep to climb out of. The arrogant monster certainly thought so there was no other reason to give me all the answers otherwise. I couldn't even call him stingy with those anymore. I just needed to ask right.

"How come sometimes there's... this dread? Even if I can't see the monster. But... not always? And other times they're perfectly terrifying, but not... in that way."

Demon seemed to know what I meant to say, even if I didn't, "We do not belong here. You know it, even if you don't understand it. The grander the discrepancy, the worse your aversion gets."

If merely standing next to a shard of that mirror does this, what would stepping onto the other side do? There go my plans for inter-dimensional travelling! Well, I suppose not my plans, but some organisations still tried to cross over... and invade them back? I didn't know what the goal there was. I'm sure they haven't thought that far either, as is often the case. After all, we had our hands pretty full here in mortal plane.

Jokes aside, that was just one more reason in long line of justifications to stay far away from all this wriggling alien mess.

I narrowed my eyes at suspiciously two-legged and two-handed specimen to wonder, "Is that why you're human-shaped? To be all logical and cuddly? Just for us? You shouldn't have." I made fun of it and even splashed with bitterness, but even I knew there were far worse silhouettes I could be hounded by.

If this was an overgrown rat with multiple mouths I probably wouldn't be just sitting here, chatting.

"Yes," the monster said and I huffed indignantly at his lack of embarrassment. Have some shame, dammit!

"Well, it's not working. I don't feel the cuddliness. Must be the horns," I shook my head, criticizing the choices of fashion again. Demon didn't care. I pushed on, "Does that mean you're terrified of us? Being entirely in an alien, incomprehensible world." "No. Mouths bypass that," he rumbled pointedly and I was delighted to find out they had a less creepy function.

"Ohh. So, they acclimatise you?"

"In a way," the air reverberated quietly.

Some unpleasant emotion tickled me and angry irritation broke out, "So... But... Why is it only humans?" I've had little basis for that accusation, but seeing Priest was enough information for my indignant self. "Can't you possess a bear or something?" I suppose I was being hypocritical again, throwing poor animals under the bus rather than no-good assholes who most likely deserved it anyway. People were trash. But as trashy as I was,

I still did not desire spending rest of my (his?) life reflecting upon the fact.

"It obviously isn't just your people. If you've assumed so, that's a fallacy on your end."

Low growl kept rolling off, "Original form means little to me. There's just so many of you," hungry child drooling at the buffet said. The tone was frankly disgusting.

So it was as simple as convenience. There had been billions of us. Truly a brimming factory farm, ripe for the reaping. But something wasn't adding up. This creature was old, that much was clear. It literally scoffed at my remaining years.

CHAPTER 9

"If you've been coming and going since the dawn of time, how come we got overrun only now?"

"Isn't it obvious?" monster drawled out.

"No?"

"You did this to yourselves. I don't know how. But now there is a hole between worlds and everyone else poured through."

"Alright. I suppose it was obvious." I agreed for it did make awful lot of sense. If it wasn't one thing, would have been another. At least this way we got to experience new tourist destinations. And perhaps even immortality, which I suspected a lot of people would line up for.

Monster's calm ticking changed into a hum, like if he was a human he'd have more to say. Partial imitation of the gesture, I suppose. "Spit it out," I urged.

"No fiery disputes?"

"I live to surprise," I shrugged with full length of my arms, but didn't really feel like playing the part of flamboyant ballerina. Flattering that the demon thought I could launch a reasonable debate against him, though.

Rubbed my icy fingers together. The talk was taking my mind off the unwanted things, but not the screaming discomfort. Walking would get my blood moving, but we were probably headed to the church town. I didn't want to get anywhere, see anyone. Including this lumbering oaf, but that was inescapable at this time.

What would be the chances of successfully ripping that skin coat of his off again? Worked out fine when I was barely coherent.

... Assault was never my thing. And to begin with, monster was unbelievably cooperative. I sauntered closer, leaned in to touch the chest and put my best seductive tone to use, "Say, what's underneath?"

There was a seam, and hints of neckline. It was definitely removable. The blanket flap had been somehow detached too.

Monster wasn't charmed or even flustered. Was not replying either. Okay, so it was a bit conceited of me to think I could temp a demon into sin of one kind or another. Nonetheless, disappointing.

"Organs," his body murmured eventually. Well, duh.

"No, I mean... under the cloak?"

There was another massive pause, but I learned to give this alien doofus a minute to mull things over. Seriously, what was so complicated here? Was he being shy? Oh my.

"Do you want to see?" monster asked quietly again and I jumped for joy.

"Yes!"

And then something unexpected happened.

"Oh," I've said, stepping away. We've been talking about entirely different things. And turns out the lengthy deliberation was well placed.

There indeed were organs, although I could not quite place them. I turned my head sideways but it didn't make any further sense from that angle either. It was like scattered puzzle, hastily stuffed back into the box and some of it possibly missing.

A bit of the mass sloshed and dribbled out on the grass. A series of cracks made me raise the eyes again. The fleshy mass twisted and crunched again. It was frankly disgusting and my own stomach started following that same flailing dance. But I could not look away.

"Did you taste so rank that something chewed on you a little and spat back out?" I could not help but wonder at the gory sight. When in panic, talk a lot to cover that up.

Couple more crunches and the insides were all gone... somewhere. Certainly nowhere in the gut cavity, nor the stomach for he didn't have one at all. It was just empty.

"The opposite," monster informed me after finishing chewing. All that was left were the haphazardly scattered sharp teeth all over the fleshy pink inside of his. The whole of abdomen cavity was a massive toothy maw. The sight was more than unsettling, I felt the dread. I wanted to run. Something very inhuman and loathsome was witnessed by my eyes and they burnt.

"Momma packed you the lunch, then? It looked delish," I gaped at the lost piece on the ground and wondered if I'm strong enough to go through with rest of the nonsense that swirled on in my mind. I certainly ate worse looking things. Picked it up... and flung it into the bushes with a yelp. "Ouch! Mama likes it a bit spicy, huh?"

Monster was growling quietly but was not saying anything still. Did not know if it was thoughtful muteness or one of abandonment. It was frankly hard to just stand here and be cornered from all sides. In thoughtful stillness, faced with an abomination, wanting to run and for everything to stop. Shuddered, looking at the still open maw. Fisted my fingers to stop them from shaking and fell forward.

The rumbling hitched from the impact. I expected the vertical jaws to slam shut, especially on that full-body twitch, but here I still was. Pricked by the teeth I fell on top of, but still living and still breathing. The smell was... not as disgusting as I imagined. Rather like a butcher shop at the city centre. Nothing but the freshest of meats. Which made sense, I suppose.

The maw around me started closing and I braced myself again, but there was no pain or terrible crunching. It just twined around my tensed back and arms, yanking me off my feet without effort. I was surprised the million needles didn't rip me apart in such a snug hold. Upon retrospection, they appeared to have gone missing altogether to that mysterious place all terrible things went.

I couldn't hear much through the pulse pounding in my ears, but steady vibration told me I wasn't missing anything. Cleared my throat to adjust the pitch of what would be undoubtedly shaky voice. "Well, do I taste as good as I look?" I asked knowing full well I must taste of well-worn sock by now.

"Accurate, as I don't have need for taste as well as the visual input."

"Soo... you... have no taste? Yea, we've already established that." How bland, I thought finding myself rolling my eyes and finally relaxing.

I was also very jealous. Most of the things I put in my mouth as a starving child and even grown adult were rancid. That also spelled out stomach pains on occasion, but since the creature could chomp on his acidic brethren like candy, that was definitely unnecessary information to him.

Horned beast did not grace me with defence on his lack of style and I started getting uncomfortable jitters again.

"My turn to taste you!" I proclaimed much braver than I felt, which was so well-practised it became a personality trait by now.

I stuck out the tongue and ran it over the glistening concave surface right in front of me, which lacked all the miniscule bony protrusions. I feared the sting of the acid too, but it wasn't there either. Which, yeah, I would have already felt on my skin.

It tasted... of nothing. Flesh was smooth in texture and there was the mucus covering it, but zest itself eluded me. Like something was definitely there, but instead it tasted of absence of flavour. Like I lacked specific buds for it. In short, it was much better than nasty.

"You do live to surprise," creature's upper chest reverberated and I found myself faced with the flat noise organ. So he did have some of those! What a delight. I suppressed a shudder.

"Is it my turn to enter you unasked?" creature spoke firmly, leaving no room for backchat. I still attempted to, as the meaning dawned upon my wide-eyed person. A tendril snaked out and brushed past my lips before I could formulate single word.

Okay, so far not as bad as I assumed. And, yes I guess that was fair. I did constantly try to stick my parts into monster's cakeholes. Was lack of asking the issue? I wondered, as my tongue snaked around the flavourless intrusion. I really wanted to ask, but work ethic took over at this time as I was nothing but professional. No talking with mouth full and all that.

The tapering feeler twirled and slipped past the tongue, into the throat. I tensed, but gag reflex was a thing of very distant past. It was going far further than usual, so it was hard to cling to any kind of normalcy. I hung suspended in a monster's mouth, tongue of whom I felt somewhere in my chest. It was so far out of my abundant atypical experiences, I did not know what to think or feel. My mind was blissfully empty for once.

I hadn't noticed how or when it was even over. I just liked my lips and realised absence of foreign objects.

"Do you feel pleasure?" I wondered out loud.

"If I want to," he'd replied.

"Do you want to?" was my only obvious inquiry.

I felt monster's grip around me relax and I was deposited back onto the firm ground again. "Later," I was told as monster stepped away to zip his flesh back up and I shuddered again. It was both from cold morning air, and the recollection he'd said exact same thing about consuming me. Figures to a monster that must have held entirely different meaning. And to begin with, what was my addled mind even suggesting there?

Thoroughly freaked out but still blissfully absentminded, I just picked a sunniest direction and walked off. It wasn't contributing towards getting any warmer after the night's damp chill and I eventually broke out of my stupor.

"Carry me!" I demanded with my arms raised towards hulking figure as I'd seen other, happier kids do at the market.

"No," monster shot it down immediately. I sighed, not in the least bit surprised. Life was never kind to my whims, no matter how small they were.

"What, why?" I grumbled stubbornly with fake surprise.

"I can walk myself," monster replicated my voice perfectly without a trace of growling or ticking. It probably was what I'd said before. Ancient beast was being so petty.

"I'm sorry, baby, that was so rude of me. I take it back," I hung off his arms and tried buttering him up with sweet-talk. No reaction.

"If you carry me..." I concentrated my entire brainpower on this. He could eat me anytime anyway, and didn't lack anything else in general. He'd been taking care of himself for literal ever. So I had nothing to offer. On the other hand... there had to be a reason I was still alive and permitted to run my loud mouth. I banked everything on curiosity. "I'll answer a question!"

There was no reaction for long-ass time again and I'd given up on the venture. I was thinking to suggest doing a request, then disregarding it completely if I got slapped with something like a don't run away again. The human hand I was still clutching on untangled itself and swept around me.

"Weeeeee!" I squealed pretending glee as I was raised up, arms up in the air and legs dangling. Perhaps if I faked hard enough... it hadn't worked even once thus far, I reflected sourly. Forced my lips to stay curled up as reality tried to force itself back in once again. No thinking about dead friends, bad brain! Concentrate on romantic getaway in countryside with a literal monster.

Wondered what would be the big question. Something he thought he couldn't just ask? Ominous. Especially after he'd just answered everything my flippant mind landed on. Of course, perhaps the timeless creature just wasn't naïve and bided its time to increase chances of an answer. Because even now, in all likelihood I'd still spout bullshit. Was this a test of character, then? To ask something obvious and see if I'd lie. Ugh, the mind games!

"Why do you force yourself to do the opposite of what your instincts demand?"

Ugh. Tough, tedious question. I swung my dangling legs and stared at the sky. The direction we walked in seems to have changed, I noted absentminded. I guessed he meant sticking my hands into his maw and the like.

"Why indeed," I muttered but what other choice did I really have? Doing the opposite of expected either amused the threat and they'd let me off, or surprised enough to give me a chance to escape.

"Suicidal and I've nothing to lose?" I eventually offered blatant and obvious answer.

"Incorrect. You've got teeth," monster informed me chillingly as though he'd extracted one or two back in the day. Subtle threat? No, not very subtle. I did not want to dwell or reflect on any of this. Buried my face within the palms, but that changed nothing. A scream was welling up inside, which would also be heard by nobody and only fuel fervour of my tormentors. Did this particular monster deserve the truth? The key to my inner workings?

"You think you can force me to do what you like with a little pain?" I scoffed and held back a flinch to this game-ending bluff. I was very malleable. It didn't take much to get me to do anything.

"Yes," monster stated simply. Wonder if that was because he'd seen me in the mansion or because the countless years taught him a thing or two about tickling under fingernails.

"Let me down," I said, starting to struggle weakly. I didn't want to talk about that, therefore wasn't entitled to this ride.

"No," monster stated and made no move to release me from firm one-handed grip.

"I wasn't threatening. Few living things could withstand what I can do," he eventually spoke. And by that I meant when the scenery has changed. Can't say my mind drifted far either. "Sometimes young humans aren't afraid, but you are. And yet you act otherwise."

"Enamoured with my impulsiveness?" I teased with a grin I didn't feel. Too exhausted to go on playing joviality I muttered, "You're not the scariest thing I've ever seen." I slumped against warm monster and stared at passing branches. "I'm sure you're terrifying as fuck and all, my cup is just full."

"But how have you survived thus far jumping head first into the danger?"

Not on my own, that's how.

"Oh look, kitties!" I pointed and flailed. Monster eventually took the hint and walked towards a band of several cats. It has been a long while since I've seen those. When he'd stopped, I looked down at the worst distraction in the world of distractions yet. There were around ten bodies lying in a ditch. Obviously whole and uneaten. One was face up and had a round hole in it. The animals stared on at us without flinching.

I looked away from the sight and found several blackened squares with charcoal poles sticking out. Unbelievable, some small community had still existed in out in the wilds not too long ago. Until.

Tried to keep it in, but couldn't resist it in the end. "See, this is scary," I said flatly. "Ancient monsters doing their thing eating one or two? That's just survival of the fittest."

"Isn't this survival of the fittest as well?" monster suggested. "Your people consume the weaker too, if they have what you want."

I shrugged, "I guess. I might just be salty from sitting on the lowest rung so much." Being powerless was such a universal sin.

Monster turned his blind head towards me in some gesture I could not decipher. "That is why I wonder how you survived. You're very well adapted. Even took down the humans of the privileged class."

He just won't leave this alone, huh. I rubbed my eyeballs and in absence of sight, the smell of rotting flesh hit me like a hammer and awoke other associations. "By dying myself!" I shouted, losing all composure. "How does that seem as winning? Great survival trait, isn't it? Is that what you want to absorb from me? Well fucking take it! Shove it and choke on it! Go hang from a tree!"

Just before I shouted some more angry nonsense I felt my head clear and anger dissipate. It was sudden and therefore very noticeable. I had no doubt monster purged those emotions, leaving me calm as the sky. Why was the weather so nice all the damn time? I wanted to get angry, be angry, but nothing was happening.

"I do not need anything from you, human. I am perfect," he paused and gave me ample time to roll my eyes. "You simply are my pet and I will take care of you, even against your wishes."

I narrowed my eyes in suspicion. Could resistance be a particular point of interest?

"Right. Well, fine. Just so you know - I am very much like a parasite. I latch onto the capable and then get them killed. You're next," I grinned venomously and tapped his chest. This wasn't a threat nor a warning. Merely a pity party for one. I would normally be better at hiding my inner workings, but monster didn't bother with repercussions and my search for boundaries continued.

The other too-human hand reached out and cupped my cheek. That, coupled with the still turned face almost made the devilish creature seem human. Almost. The gestures were still fixed and uncanny. "That is acceptable," he said gruffly.

CHAPTER 10

Just a day later I saw spires of the bell towers. All my meandering delayed the inevitable only by that much.

It was the first time I observed it from afar and the fortified town wasn't anything outstanding in appearance. The colourful roofs screamed how beloved the properties had been back in the day. When I squinted I could almost imagine how it all must have looked all those years ago with fresh paint, neat hedges and blooming gardens. A scene from a life I never had a chance of living even then.

Now though, most everything was dimmed or even on the cusp of collapse. A lot of the previously quaint houses were dismantled and bricks donated to the unsightly yet essential perimeter wall. Barren, gravelly lots where houses used to stand both on the inside and outside the protected territory. Gaping eyeholes of some abandoned cottages, as glass must have been even harder to come by out here than in the city.

I saw some movement beyond the wall from my high perch. Sentries noticed the demon approach. He was sticking out like a sore thumb on these plains, after all. Good for them not to be napping on this fine day.

I saw people lurk at the entrance, waiting for the approach, but demon wasn't following the road exactly and just leaped over the wall like complete savage. I'm guessing that was expected, or they'd have moved to open the gates. He stopped at the small central square and I was gracefully deposited onto the cobblestones. Several denizens already stood waiting, couple more trailing in. Few eyes peered out of the former prayer house's dark gateway. Quite the crowd of curious gawkers.

"Greetings, fellow dark cultists! I have returned. Oh and him," I looped thumb vaguely behind me. My voice was sonorous and clear, posture proud and mighty. Whatever I wanted to pull off, I did it. There was no doubt.

"The fuck is he wearing," some grump muttered loud enough for everyone to hear.

I wasn't to be cowed. "Glad you've addressed the issue immediately. Your god commands this be our new uniform," I bellowed the decree without as much as twitching my lips. More than few sets of eyes popped out. The god in question did not confirm or deny. Excellent.

All the horrified glancing around told me I was sufficiently believable. Being carried in like a foreign prince must have done the heavy lifting, but still. Nobody argued. Great success.

"That said, the uniform is hardly weather appropriate. You," I pointed at the asshole with deepest scowl, "bring me a coat." As warm as the breeze was, it still managed to shrivel me up so much I was almost appropriate again.

Guy cast a glance towards the unseeing demon, then back at me and I waved him off impatiently. I'll probably get shanked later if the reddening expression was any indicator, but five minutes of authority? Totally worth it.

Everyone else just stood and waited, both wary and in awe. Just like the last time. Crossed my arms and stared back at them, too. They've never seen a monster? You'd think out here in the boonies it would be the opposite. Or was it truly some sort of religious experience for the lot? Almoner swore it wasn't, but

I still couldn't help but wonder. Some could have still carried sentiments of looking for meaning in weird places. Some could have freshly gained it. The creature was probably older than our entire existence. Were they, the monsters, all like that?

"That thing you ate, was it as old as you?" I asked staring up at the curling horns.

Monster didn't reply and I thought that maybe there was just one village fool he spoke to at a time. Was this why everybody flocked to witness it, rather than engaging themselves? Low grumble dismissed my musings, "Too young to know better."

"So you eat babies," I skipped several questions that popped up in favour of poking fun.

"Yes."

The low bark made several people flinch and I sighed. This guy was a terrible stand-up comedian.

"So how young is too young? How do your usual lunches compare to you and each other? Or humans."

"Humans are my usual lunch," demon growled out and now I was sure he had an agenda to ruin my fun. Or perhaps he didn't enjoy an audience? Or did, but had other ideas of entertainment? He was posing as god to these people, incidentally or not. Had an image to uphold or whatever. Looks like my new goal in life will be to ruin that!

Before I could get to business, mean-faced man returned with a raggedy coat, which he also vindictively dragged through the mud. Which was fine by me, since I was the least fussy orphan in our corner of town. Which apparently wasn't cute anymore in a grown-ass man, in Cherry's opinion. Vanquishing chill that threatened to settle over my heart with a massive smile, I grabbed at the garb and tucked myself in. Finally, some warmth! No more huddling with an ancient terror for basic survival.

Priest trailed just behind the big surly. Demon spoke before he could be greeted, "There is a group of thirty eight humans just outside of your domain. Two very close, very quiet."

Dead-eyed battle monk nodded slowly, "They got here yesterday. I'm waiting on their move."

That was bad news, no matter which way sliced. Nobody just showed up to lurk at your doorstep with good intentions. They had to be well-armed to just camp among the trees too.

All of that sounded terrific, so I gave the crowd thumbs up and made myself scarce. Priest's intense stare probably attempted to keep me nailed to the ground, but I was a free spirit. Or at least I was going to pretend so for as long as I can get away with it.

As the scary-looking mob began discussing unpleasantries on their doorstep, I was thrilled to avoid it completely. Especially since I was familiar with the layout this time around and didn't need any help getting around. First order of business! Warm bath.

Scenery was plainly idyllic. The old opulent building stood majestic to one side, the river sloshed down the hill on its merry way. It was still relatively early in the day, so nobody else was washing up. Some carpenter with two right arms put up the shower stalls, benches and even saunas skilfully. Everything was beautiful and not least bit crooked. Great communal recreation area, even if I didn't see joining the local crowd.

Most of the city had just cold running water, which was frankly miracle enough. The house we unlawfully occupied had even that turned off. We found workarounds, but it was still tedious and not least bit pleasant undergoing. Especially on occasions when officials bothered to check if anybody was stealing their shit. Long story short, I was ecstatic to take a dip in a heated river water. I was okay at kindling a fire, so it didn't even take long. Several cranks of a lever and I jumped right in onto the wooden rack inside the metal bathtub without bothering to undo the straps. They were hardly in the way, anyway.

After finally warming up my cold bones, felt an intense hunger. My body was starting to relax. The bunch of tiny wild pears I'd picked up for breakfast were hardly satisfying. Much less so than the instance of annoying demon to go back and get them.

I could take a casual stroll through their vegetable patch, but I saw myself being watched by several scowls already. It would be an easily provoked fun, but for once I just didn't feel like it. I was too damn tired. And fortunately for everyone who would be involved, going on empty was the standard for me. I took a couple of turns in the small town and ducked away from view into someone's beloved rose bushes to nap in the waning sun.

When I woke up the stars were twinkling. My back was frozen over again because of the cool earth. Bad choices on my part again, but nothing new there either. As I sat up, found blanket draped on top of myself.

"Grandma loved these roses," familiar young cadence spoke. I seemed to have startled Almoner out of some reverie. He smiled but unlike when I did it, it was all grief. He'd need more practise with this. I grabbed around until I found his frozen fingers and gripped them.

My foggy mind grappled for ideas. "Yea? They... did look splendid. Didn't think I'd be seen through the thicket."

Blond head jerked to the side to point at a window. Frankly, I hoped this was one of the abandoned houses. It should have been, technically, as Almoner stayed in church... while I was around anyway. I must have caught him in a bout of melancholy. Might as well, misery did love company.

"Are you okay?" he asked suddenly, after taking firm hold of my hand. "The devil... has found you again."

I chewed on my lip, moved by insistent sincerity in the young voice. This sweet summer child of mine. "I'm sorry for not saying anything before leaving. There... wasn't time." There probably was, but I didn't want to take risks. I was selfish like that.

His other hand flailed to dismiss it, "I understand completely. That's fine. I hoped... you'd get back home to your family safe." I don't think I flinched or showed anything on my face. I had too much practise to be read easily. But his eyes scrutinised my face in the dark anyway and at that moment I felt seen through completely. He said eventually, "You didn't answer."

Ah, evading was the mistake. I could be flippant, but felt like I owed this boy more than that. He did take care of my lame ass that entire week for me to just disappear like smoke. "I... am not okay. Not remotely," I admitted impassively, fearful that the admission alone would break the dam. In the companionable stillness some pressure released and I felt that maybe I could do even a little better. "They are dead," I whispered out the cold hard facts and didn't even break to bits. I thought it would hurt more, but turns out I accepted the reality for what it was days ago. I was as low as I could have gone already.

Almoner exhaled so deep he was about to implode. "Because of... the..." he finally stammered out and I shook head, understanding the glaring concerns.

"I don't even fully understand how he'd ended up where I was. Completely unrelated." Just look at me being cool and nonchalant about massively uncomfortable, life-defining events.

"That's... good?"

I shrugged, having no idea. I didn't appreciate being ripped out of the maw of blissfulness, but good for the kid, I suppose. The idol remains untarnished for little while longer.

"Never mind all that! Say, where do you people keep the fuel? I'm going on another trip," I inquired cheerfully, glossing over all the unpleasantries. I knew where they kept the cars, which littered the abandoned roads by the dozen, but important resources weren't sitting out in the open.

My palm got gripped so tight it was almost painful. "You mustn't do that," youth informed me, his shadowed face was fixed upon mine, although he couldn't have seen much either. Before I could protest and insist, Almoner went on, "They wouldn't want to become reason for it. Don't burden them so."

My mouth opened several times as I imitated a suffocating fish. No, there was nothing I could say. He'd completely seen through me. This darkness worked against me.

"The dead don't care," I shot back with venom. Shook my head, wanting to say he doesn't, wouldn't understand. But there was nothing special about it. Mine was generic old story. We're all just playing same old twisted game where nobody wins.

He was correct, I realised. Ruby would slog me unconscious if he knew I was actively trying to waste all his effort of keeping me alive all those years. Really, the man should have invested it differently. Perhaps if that busybody hadn't began picking stays up starting with me, he wouldn't have gone down that sad route at all. There really was no point of me having been alive at all. I found myself pressing the fingers into the wet eyes as if to gouge them out.

"I'm not dead," Almoner's hands gripped my wrists to pull them away just as I started drawing blood and forced me to look at pale outline of the blond head. Damn kid was surprisingly good at this. Not quite the naïve brat he'd seemed to be in daylight. Village healer for a reason, it would seem.

So I'd kissed him. It was likely an overused routine which he'd relayed to every sad sod around - of which there were many nowadays - but I was cheap anyway. He implied and I needed to forget the things he'd dredged up. It all checked out as a go in my head.

The blonde's tongue was sluggish and timid. He hadn't done this a lot, which I'd found surprising he wasn't that much younger than me. It was saying more about me than him and I listened to every word. What has all that been for? All those people...

His fingers tentatively brushed my hairless chest and my companion snorted lightly, "What is it you're wearing this time?"

"Don't worry, you're gonna love it," I assured him with a smirk, shrugging out of the coat.

"Was this what they were whispering about?" Almoner chuckled to himself, his palm brushing over the leather straps one by one.

When I moved to get closer, the blonde started to put his arms around me but suddenly pulled away, landing the hands on my shoulders this time.

"What?" I asked sensing irritability returning. He couldn't have been that inexperienced. Or was small town boy remembering he's not into men?

"You know I like you," he begun and looked for words above my head.

"But?" I urged instead of agreeing. This was going somewhere I didn't need right now and I was done with all the suspenseful pauses that suddenly befell my life.

"You seem to belong to the devil," blonde whispered choppily.

"So do you?"

Youth shook his blond mane. "Not like that. He doesn't even talk to anyone besides Priest. And even with him, devil just walks away without a care no matter how badly he's mangled."

"Well, that's because... well, for one Priest is immortal and..." they're connected in some way anyway. There was more I could say on the subject, but didn't feel like going into it right now. The kid was just looking for an excuse anyway. "Why would an alien creature even have such concept? He watched me get railed all night long and didn't care. If you don't want to, just grow up and say so," I said with a knowing smirk and patted Almoner on the cheek. I felt his face contort from frown into a surprise and confusion. Introducing more oddities into already stupefied mind might have been a mistake.

"Those people... are they alive?" kid asked stiffly and I didn't react. It was unrelated bit of murder on my part anyway.

I groaned tiredly and chose to address the other thing instead. Monster carried more authority anyway. Strange he had stuck around, but the armed threat to his little slice of paradise must have been a reason enough. "Monster!" I called out into the dead of night and cringed for it was loud, then repeated, "Ey, monster!"

There was no reply. I had no doubt ancient monster could hear lone bellow in the night. And probably not just that, but the entire half-whispered conversation. Those ears were seriously out of proportion with rest of the body. Almoner gripped me by the straps and shook as I was about to shout more, with his horrified eyes obvious even in the dark. I chuckled. As fun as the spectacle could have been, I didn't really want everyone up in my business either.

"Fine, I'll go ask like a cultured person," I sighed for show and stood. "Where's he at?"

"By the church," shaky healer replied, his hands not relaxing nor releasing the straps. Not until I kissed him again. Then I'd left him standing in the shadow, stepping onto the path outlined by solar powered torches here and there. It was meagre but they did the job. If the village people needed actual light they'd set fire to blackened intestines of some monsters. They burned well and brightly. Seeing as all the ritzy doohikeys took a turn towards decline, the alternative advancements would probably end up taking over in the long term.

And I even knew where they kept that barrel. File the idea for later.

Frolicking down the street I regretted leaving my coat behind. The nights were getting chilly. But that's not what was on my mind at the time. Seeing demon's dark silhouette emerge from behind the corner I squealed and launched myself at him in a sprint, "Baby! Where've you been? I've missed you so!" He stood exactly where I'd left him. Probably same exact spot.

From mere steps away I lunged, shouting, "Catch me!"

Instead of flopping down on the stone pavement, or toppling over us both and landing in a heap of elbows, I was caught and hung suspended.

"You actually did," I exhaled surprise. I'd usually trip everybody down and Ruby would then add onto the new bruises.

"Of course," monster ticked quietly as though it was only obvious. Show off.

"Sooo, did you eavesdrop?" I inquired knowing the answer full well.

"I heard, yes."

"So why didn't you broadcast your permission for everyone to know? You're scaring the common folk into being unreasonable, yano."

"You assume much," demon chastised and I raised my eyebrow.

"Is that a no?"

"No."

Demon didn't elaborate and my irritation made a comeback. I swung my dangling legs up and down, to calm myself. The few dim blips aside, the surroundings drowned in the dark. The scarce torches weren't all that visible from distance. Stars above were only intensifying the feeling of being somewhere deep in the ocean. It was terrifyingly beautiful.

"What's your name anyway? I'd hate to have some other monster pop up next time I need to holler."

"Your kind has given me many names," horned monster rumbled.

I haven't seen all that many movies, but still recognised the line. I scoffed deeply irritated, "I didn't ask that. What you call yourself?"

"I do not," he said and I felt my nails rake something. There wasn't pain so it must not have been my skin, but monster haven't reacted either. Must be nice to be able to turn off every bothersome function of your body.

Released abused flesh and made a fist instead. Fine, the monster was right. I didn't call myself either, was not that crazy yet. Before I could specify further, monster elaborated, "Speech is distinctly human mode of communication. It's inefficient."

I huffed at the stuck-up monster - of course his way was much better. Didn't protest with my inept words however, because deep down I knew he was probably correct. These things had eons to work it all out.

Tendril separated itself from a hem of his hood and twined around my neck. I tensed up. Unsettling, but the creature could rip me apart without this. Base of my skull tickled and between blinks I started knowing more. The buildings suddenly were clear as day, and I saw far further. Forest, the people in it. The swaying branches around them. The critters on the other side. The entirety of information made the tiny personality within my meat suit balk.

A powerless gargle in lieu of words focused the attention back onto us and the onslaught of information stopped immediately. I shook, revolted and exhausted. If I had any strength left, I'd leap away and retch. The negative physical sensations disappeared few heartbeats later but I still hung, breathing heavy and nobody said a thing.

That wasn't even one set of information. When I made noise the image diverged and I realised I was thrown into another detailed landscape. The later one was present. The previous must have been from when we came in. Had he tried to relay something? Things had been somewhat different, but I just didn't have any spare capacity to compare.

If monsters could assault their conversational partners with the grand totality of anything and everything, no wonder they didn't waste their breath. Speech was quite inadequate after all. Too bad that was all our puny human brains were capable of.

After what must have been way too long I snapped back and looked into the fishbowl of darkness once again. What were we talking about again? Right. Names.

"So when somebody calls you, they send you an image of you?"

"No..." This time I felt the monster try and put complicated things into a small one-sentence package for my little brain to comprehend and didn't fault him. I did decide to fault him when it seemed horned devil abandoned that explanation whatsoever and moved on from it. Eventually the chest rumbled, "Such intrusion is not usually welcome. Too easy to kill. By accident or on purpose."

I sniffled what could probably be blood and hissed, "What, too intrusive? If only there were other ways to casually shout from a distance." Stupid monsters.

There was another ponderous pause and he said, "My name is under your fingernails."

"What?" I stared at the unclenched fist, obviously not seeing a damned thing.

"The smell is specific to each individual living thing."

"You people are so damn complicated," I huffed out, rubbing my temple. Gave my nails a whiff. It smelled of the ground I've been gripping in my nap.

"It's the first time you called us people," monster stated.

"Aw, what, lil baby monster had his feelings hurt?" I mocked him for no reason besides my own defensiveness. I didn't really spend all that much time pondering the subject before leaving the city, none at all to be exact, but then at least one of them appeared and spoke. It was simple to come to right conclusions.

"No. Humans are less than bugs to us." And yet he brought it up and that told me something.

"Oh, don't be so butthurt. Plenty of humans are monsters too," I explained hastily and went back to dissecting more interesting things.

"So this smell... Fresh meat?" There was barely anything on my hands, but I vividly recalled what his maw smelled like. I grasped for polite way to say it was generic as fuck. "I'm probably not picking it up right... All innards smell more or less like that. Right? Perfume or hints of oil would be more specific to tell people apart, no? Or whatever it is you'd be around the most."

"Items and environment add clarifying markers, but they aren't the essence. Human senses are hardly sufficient to tell most of those apart."

I inhaled deep but there was nothing still. Not even on his living coat. Which was odd, and how did I not notice it earlier? Well, I guess it would be somewhat weird to be carrying tantalising fragrance of butcher shop everywhere you went. I didn't walk around with my ID taped to the forehead either.

That took a lot of effort and I still didn't have a name. Now I of course understood his side of issue, but it hardly helped. "So how do I call you? If you make me pick something, I promise you it shan't be flattering, Hammie."

Monster ticked away quietly and then said, "I primarily smell of nerve tissue."

"Hmm... Fitting, as you do get on my nerves a lot. Brainiac? Highbrow?" I pondered. That went with the body parts theme the monsters had going, but these were far too flattering. "Noodle!"

"You sound malnourished," monster bit back and I had to admit he was probably right.

"Fine, you do deserve a normal, human name. Shall we call you Parkinson? In honour of all that restless twitching you do," I said and nodded energetically. This could really grow on me.

"Why didn't you eat?" creature asked after a short tingling sensation I was learning to associate with him doing something to me.

"Stop that," I demanded, yanking myself forward to interrupt whatever that's been happening on my back. It ceased and didn't restart even when I settled back. Why was I still lounging in his arms anyway? It was warmer, I suppose.

"Eat, or I will do it for you," monster stated. He knew I didn't like that. We've covered that extensively during the trip.

Commands didn't sit right with me at all and I frowned in disgust. Almost forgot the creature was as bad as all the rest of the power-tripping assholes. There goes all the rapport we've almost established. No matter, he will be able to be as bossy as he wants to the pile of my ash soon.

"Of all the things, that's what I need you doing least," I muttered angrily and scrambled off the alien overlord.

Monster let me go easily for once, but his hand lingered and brushed upwards as he asked, "What do you need me to do?" It felt undeservedly pleasant and a shiver emanated from his touch and down my spine. It confused me. Was I that starved of tender touches? Yes, but no. As natural as it felt, this couldn't be coincidence, with a monster that smelled primarily of nerves. I stared up at the blind horns. That was... suggestion. Right?

One way to find out for sure. "Again," I demanded. One way or the other I came here looking for some bliss. Did it matter I'd find it in hands of literal monster? Not in the slightest.

CHAPTER 11

I loitered most of the following day. We ate breakfast and Almoner ran off to do a shift on the wall. It was still cold outside so I opted for more warm bed time. After finally catching up on all my beauty sleep I crawled out of the aged abode and ventured to see what other common folk were up to.

I saw quite a number of them walk around with riffles on their back and felt sudden urge to go back and bury my head in the pillow.

Braving the cracked up pavement regardless, I found out that the wry stares I was getting weren't imagined which was odd. I even wore an ordinary t-shirt for once. Nevertheless, I was happy to finally stumble upon some normalcy. I waved to a couple of frowning women. Smiled blindingly at the scowling gangbangers. I could almost affix familiar faces from the city onto these people. The more things changed, the more they stayed the same.

Sadly, not all were leering from a distance.

"... And now you crawl out of that brat's place," a pushy nuisance spoke at me again and yet again I ignored him. I didn't like this particular specimen from the last visit, but then the brazen asshole wasn't bothering me directly. Perhaps I was worth the effort now that my face wasn't all swollen. "I knew..."

I turned and jumped up in pretend surprise. Right on time too - his paw was about to land on my shoulder. "Oh, good lord, say something next time!" I exclaimed.

Hefty man's eyes narrowed, unsure if I was insulting or just not entirely here. Some days I wasn't sure either. He settled on me being daft in favour of achieving his goal, "Shall we go to my place?"

Such an everyday suggestion. Better, even, as my usual place of business was an alley or a literal hole in the wall. And yet, there was no reason for me to be living that life anymore. I rocked on my heels, grinning. "And why would I do that?" I asked befuddled.

The arm ended up slung over my shoulder anyway. "Oh, don't play coy. I knew you were the type since I first saw you," sleazebag whispered to my ear. I didn't ask for details. I probably did look every bit of what I was. This was essentially just another brash client, I just didn't have the need for money any more.

I wish I had cigarettes to light up and pretend he wasn't here again. Perhaps I could pull one out of his pocket? Man's other hand landed to pat my chest and interfered with the grand plans. He insisted once again, "I can show you good time, you won't regret it."

Turns out I was ignoring him like a champ even without a prop. I sighed, because it was tiresome being so good at escaping my problems one way or the other. Or making them worse. It was dice roll.

I scoffed with genuine amusement. Tapped my lips with a finger, pretending to be in deep though and said, "Highly doubt that." As his grip tightened, I went on, "First of all, I would be showing you good time." The confused man stopped squeezing my nape. I shrugged with my pondering arm, purposefully aggravating the guy some more. "But why would I? I mean look at yourself. When was it you even shaved? Or, oof, washed?"

"Listen here, you whore," the other arm of his gripped my throat, but the amateur was terrible at this and my voice box was free to keep throwing insults.

I nodded along, "Hookers are your only hope of getting laid." I was too tired to be on my best behaviour and frankly several bruises would have done good job of reminding me to occasionally shut up. This wasn't a guy who'd take a simple no for an answer anyway. I'd have to demolish him, make him truly loathe the sight of me.

In a flash everything changed - and not for the worse. Mild shock. I blinked and found the man lying on the pavement and another standing over him. The dead eyes bore into me accusingly. Or with constipation. I had no idea.

"Hiii," my energetic wave was accompanied by a pitched greeting. Having already said everything I planned to, I turned and walked off. I already hated this day. Should have just gone back and napped.

"I met a very pale, very upset red headed rapist," toneless words caught up to me but didn't register immediately and I kept walking. Then they did and angry annoyance flared up.

"He's not... What?" Was all I managed as I turned on my heel and stared, unable to hope.

"Had you not gone into hiding yesterday, I would have told you sooner," Priest explained crossing his arms and staring. He was being accusatory, then.

"Had you had more than two expressions, I may have gotten clearer clue," I retorted.

"Two?" he asked seeming almost intrigued, but I didn't feel like cracking pooping jokes all of a sudden. If they met it had to be after I was taken.

"When?" I asked, clenching my fingers to stop them from shaking.

"Earlier yesterday. He handed me a bag of supplies and promised me more if I knew anything about your whereabouts," tired-looking man in charge recounted in complete monotone. "Thanks for the supplies, by the way."

I fell onto my knees, muttering, "He's alive?"

"Barely," Priest said impassively and an image popped into my head of forlorn redhead forcing himself to move through the pain and bleeding stitches to find a way out. He was always so unstoppably stubborn. I had to get back before he hurt himself more, because he would.

"I... need to go," I muttered to nobody in particular and scrambled up to stumble in a vague direction of the city, cutting though someone's yard. I would jack a car, but I couldn't drive. I needed to move anyway. Physically do something about this.

"You plan on walking," deadpan tone ridiculed my choices from several steps away. "You smell like us now but you're not a mouth, are you?"

I glanced over my shoulder, astounded by proclamation. Thank fuck for the little miracles. "Now why would you say something so hurtful?"

Priest stared at me and I turned away. It was too piercing to bear. The demon would probably don this exact vast emptiness on his face if it was ever revealed.

"Scent can only do so much. There has to be intelligence to be warned off by it, or a nose to catch it in first place. You won't make far," I was quietly informed.

"No, you stink!" I pointed at him indignantly and worriedly glanced towards the church and outdoorsy amenities.

Soundlessly following man kept talking, "Parts of your body have been replaced. That's not gonna wash off."

I grit my restored teeth and squeezed fists, stopping hands from rubbing together to reassure myself they were really mine. "Why do you care anyway?" I hissed at him.

"Chance are he'll follow you to make sure you live and I might need help with the interlopers," man in charge admitted solemnly.

"Didn't you get them already? What was with all the noise whole morning?" The distant crackle of gunfire on full auto roused me irrevocably, and the bastards didn't even have decency to be all dead. Rude.

Priest's eyes kept boring into my soul as he spoke, "Something else has found them. Since they don't need to pretend they aren't here anymore, I expect some progress today. So if you pipe down and wait a bit, I'll drive you back myself."

"Ugh, why didn't you just go in and kill them days ago?" I muttered, annoyed about this inconvenience. There was about zero chance they were here on peace mission.

"Because there're a lot of machine guns and I'd need to gorge incessantly to replace what I lose," he informed me unenthusiastically. That was a lot of information and I wondered if townspeople who badgered him got this exact answer or was I privy to family secrets now.

I shrugged and whispered conspiratorially, "I prefer to slack off 'til the last minute, too."

"Your rapist buddy will be fine. He had horde of kids and women telling him to sit down," Priest looked off into the direction city was at, too.

"Not like he listens," I muttered and scowled in remembrance of his words. "You call him that again and you'll wake up to nasty surprises in your boots."

"Terrifying," his dead fish stare landed back on me. It would be, I silently pledged. I was of no use in a brawl, but I'd teach this oddball the horror of anticipation. "They ran out of other brands at the fair?" the intense man asked coarsely and I stared back at the local overlord. He had to be shrewd to deserve the position and likely was much older than he looked. Priest knew when he saw a killer. Was that astute man's way of being placating? Such a wise elder.

"Something like that," I muttered, boxing up my ideas of being minor menace. For now. "I'll be around," I promised vaguely and walked off, away from the shortcut towards wilderness.

CHAPTER 12

Plopped down next to gloomy-looking Almoner. He pretended to smile in a greeting. It didn't seem like just the mind-numbing boredom of an eight hour shift which must be coming to its end by now. Lingering yesterday's melancholy? Worry about the imminent attack? The gossip flying around town? Divine retribution? Secrets? So many problems to choose from. I ignored all of them.

And created my own. "I stole all your strawberry jam and you'll have to fight me for it," I announced mischievously.

Almoner was unperturbed, but the grin seemed happier, "No, you didn't." This confidence made me think that I had in fact overlooked something.

"The cellar," I said suspensefully, "is now empty."

Brawny blondey snorted, "No, it isn't." I was about to weave more lies, but he interrupted me with a permission, "You're welcome to it anyway, boney."

I pretended to be insulted, he pointed out how loose his clothes were on me. With such light-hearted banter we successfully kept our worries at bay, neither mentioning anything relevant. Sun started weighing heavy on the horizon and a bell sounded. Few seconds later a radio crackled, telling about an odd couple at one of the gates asking to talk to leadership.

I wanted to sit tight and miss out on the excitement, but at that exact moment shift change came and relieved Almoner. Since the kid wasn't yet cured of his youthful curiosity, we made our way towards one of the gates.

Plenty of armed friendlies gathered here to gawk. It was an overkill for mere two patiently waiting silhouettes.

The fortification was a little above my head, but there were mounds every few steps to... observe and fire back? I couldn't resist peeking over it either. The strangers wore camouflage. Clean and shaved. Didn't look like they spent days camping out in the woods, fighting off monsters. They were armed too, but stood relaxed. The bad news were, these people didn't look like bandits.

There wasn't much to speak of that way. Some saplings and an unused road. Even I could tell these people circled around. Will the assault start from the other side, then? Perhaps it was good choice to position myself at an opposite wall.

"What do you want?" a guy who wasn't Priest called back. Envy. He hung around the man often enough for me to think that maybe he did have the authority to do this. Surely everybody else thought so for nobody said a thing. This guy was older, perhaps oldest I have seen in the settlement. He wore leather jacket with patches, black bandana and sunglasses. The very image of Priest's biker crew, although I was yet to see any motorcycles.

"I am captain Spengla. I am empowered by our government to assess your settlement," taller of the questionable men shouted. "We are here to help."

"We don't need yer help," the gramps called back loudly.

They argued the point back and forth for bit, military man offering food, possible restoration of running water, sewage and electricity. The old man didn't give any details about just how fine the little town got by without any of those. And they truly did. Waste went into compost heaps, water came from the wells and lighting from the beeswax and alien innards. Whatever else they needed they successfully traded for.

"It is time we stood united, not scattered each to his own. You are still part of the country," soldiers implored, their approach changing towards appeals to a better human nature. There was none to be had. Faces around me were all frowning. We all knew what that really meant.

"Nice euphemism for taxes, but we aren't making any money," old coot said. Cash, of course, was the least interesting thing in a harsh world of hunger and survival. "Or does the local lord mandates we have to give up half of our potatoes now? Welcome back to feudalism, boys!" Villagers laughed grimly. They too thought granary was point of interest in this inspection. They weren't graced by thugs, but it was close enough.

"We do not need your help," he reiterated after commotion died off. "Nor are we able to assist you or the others. We have just enough for ourselves. Leave."

The tall fighter did not relent, "You misunderstand. There are many ways to cooperate. You could operate as a safe house for travelling convoys or provide intelligence on surrounding areas. We could open a regular trade route. New documents could be issued and passages opened to urban centres." That suddenly did seem like a good deal. Tad too good and it immediately made me suspicious by default.

"We could go into cities?" somebody asked loudly in a slew of hushed whispers.

"Of course. You are our citizens," the captain confirmed fervidly.

Odd. On both sides. Getting into a city wasn't that hard. Perhaps the bumpkins never tried because of the long trek to reach one? And military men thought too highly of their impenetrable defences? Because nobody ever checked identities of those already inside. Branded people were the only ones to get the occasional boot.

"Who's that guy?" I asked Almoner and he did confirm the intrigued speaker was one of their own. Priest's fellow, picked up out the wastes before they even got here.

"You think it's a bad idea?" healer asked and I shrugged. Really didn't have an opinion.

"I grew up in place ran by military. Their shenanigans would seem normal to me. But..." I concentrated and gave it a big think. "They probably intend to leave a garrison permanently. To ensure safety of their whatever. You'd have to do what person with a gun tells you to. And they wouldn't let just anyone walk around like that," I gestured towards the armed crowd. Some wore brands. Yeah, definitely not these fellows. But even now the villagers just listened to scary-looking motherfuckers who would sack them in the teeth for nasty look, so would it really be all that different?

Old man deliberated with his cronies and must have reached a similar conclusion. "However beneficial your offer is, we do not want strangers traipsing around. Nor your assistance necessary."

"Is that because of the mouth who lives here?"

Chilling quiet extinguished the whispers. Even the idiots were catching up that something was not quite what it seemed here, in case they missed a memo of war band watching them from afar.

"What do you mean?" old man feebly played senility card. His scratchy voice certainly assisted with the illusion, even if the strong frame denied it. The enemy didn't see it.

"We have a report of a man defeating foreign entity, then flipping van back and driving here."

"Ah... you mean travelling merchant? We have nothing to do with that."

"And what about the other mouth? One with horns." Our number was up. They began revealing their cards.

Gut-wrenching tension was present and I couldn't hold back, especially since nobody else had any handy excuses on hand, "That's just our Parkinson. He's going through a phase." The crowd gaped at me some with horror, others just frowning. I shrugged, whispering the explanation to them, "You know, because of the..." I exaggerated tremors on my hands for show. Several frowns turned into pity or disgust and I rolled my eyes. These god damn bumpkins understood nothing.

"We mean no harm to you or your... allies. But we are coming in and assessing the settlement," military man stated. "For one, you are restricting passage through public lands. Two, as stated, you still are part of this country and we must ensure the laws are being abided to."

"Three, take our food!" one of the crowd yelled at the sunset.

"That is entirely unimportant right now. I am tasked to make a census and accurate map of land we realistically hold."

"Census? For conscription," another irritated voice called out.

"It's strictly voluntary service. However, once you hear of the benefits, you will be lining up to do your duty," captain whatshisname was still being diplomatic but tone of his voice changed to more authoritative. Nice to meet you, I thought.

"Which way did you come from?" I asked, not really caring for the answer it was all too easy to lie. But part of me wanted to find out anyway. Some frowning people gave me stares again.

After getting the answer, I deliberated geography with Almoner and decided soldier was vague enough to either be truthful or lie and get away with it. Which was answer enough.

"Captain something," I called back.

"Spengla," man replied calm and collected. He really liked his name. Soldier boy was either really an official on official business or about to smear someone's reputation with terrible atrocities. But that's a lot of work and dedication, so probably the former. Why have someone else ruin your good name, if you can do it yourself?

"Why such shallow graves?" I poked my head out to look at the pair again. I wouldn't be able to tell if they lied, but there was a chance to catch them off guard and slipping up. "And didn't even finish burying the bodies. Tsk tsk tsk. Why such a rush?"

"What bodies?" No reaction. My supreme hit and run interrogating techniques were powerless against these professionals.

The two whispered among themselves with completely relaxed postures whilst waiting. I had no further inquiries, villagers frowned at their brand new and shiny madman.

The awkward lull in the talks must have told soldiers we have no more questions. "We will come back again tomorrow and expect to be welcomed inside. It will happen one way or the other. Order will be re-established. We are giving you this night to talk amongst yourselves and get used to the idea. We can iron out the details afterwards. Have a good night." The two turned and walked back briskly.

Whilst some descended into chatter amongst themselves, one of the crowd snarled at me and strode as though to shove or punch. "What was that about? You think it's some kind of joke?"

I wasn't about to find out which option he'd prefer. Ran on first sign of trouble. Could have mouthed off some more, but getting beat up by a gang and a mob didn't seem quite as fun as being able to painlessly breathe. Someone was still giving chase and I sped up. It wasn't Almoner because the kid still argued with those that felt too lazy to go after actual reason of their ire. Welp. I guess, I was a little too used to my companions being able to scram.

The people who chased after me weren't as good at this as me and I was gaining distance, but the town was only so big. I really didn't want to brave the wilderness at night. Swerved, vaulted a little unkempt hedge and flattened myself to the ground to hide. My legs carried me to seek safety in the presence of someone bigger and badder. My pursuers perhaps lost me, but likely just figured out where I went. Nobody even crossed the street to get into demon's face. Ha, fools! The creature would just stand by and watch me getting beat up again. Luckily, they didn't know that and I have sown enough doubts.

I sighed and turned over to lay on my back, staring at the dimming sky.

He was alive. He was alive.

"Household in the woods was not eradicated by these particular humans," demon's growl rolled off the cold stone and through my back. I rubbed my face tiredly. Of course. Should have just let them kick me unconscious and spare everybody the misery of my musings. He went on, "but they knew who you were talking about."

"Knew as in found it like that?" I checked.

"Knew names."

That didn't prove anything, neither had it laid the suspicions to rest. Quite the opposite.

I blankly stared at the cloudy red sky again. This information didn't serve me in any way at all whatsoever. Such unnecessary bit of detail. I didn't even know why I bothered asking. I knew the soldiers would be coming in and establishing dominance here anyhow and that was already reason enough for the village to fight back, which they were willing to do in first place. There was only ever us or them. And I wasn't part of this anyhow. My people were out there.

I found my vision obstructed by my own fingers and before I could rake my face again, donned a smile and turned to gawk at the horned statue in the shadow of grandeur house of worship.

"Why are you outside anyway?" I asked to get my mind off things. I really barely cared. Monster could sail himself down the stream if that made him happy. Surely would improve my mood and situation. All the villagers who suddenly took liking to the side entrances would appreciate it too.

"I am not human," demon grouched out slowly. "I do not need to eat or sit down."

"But you do need to. Eat," I countered with some distaste.

"Only if I move a lot," demon explained solemnly.

Circle of life. There goes that attempt at conversation. Work, stupid brain. Work on something that's not depressing. And something that didn't involve yesterday - because I wanted to come closer. To put my palms on the rough leather. The urge for that was unexpected and unreasonable, so I chased it off.

"You'll turn to stone if you keep this up. I mean, look, people already started thinking you're a statue and leaving flowers like it's some memorial," I said looking straight into the mess at his clawed boots. There were couple of candles, too. Apparently not everybody avoided the demon. I lamented the fact that I wasn't the one to think of this. The scene was genius.

Priest's stealthy form quietly popped out of nowhere. This seemed a lot like business and I didn't care about that. I jumped onto my feet and went to look for more of the meaningless crap for the demon's altar. Do they have a funeral wreath somewhere in there? No, probably not. I'd need to pick those flowers myself, at least there were a lot of overgrown gardens nearby. Ribbons?

Stepped inside the oppressive structure and breathed the cooler air. Sun wasn't able to permeate these solid walls, barely casting colourful light through the narrow high-set windows. Some people lounged around. Quite a number of them. In time of danger everyone relocated here, after all. They stared at the unwelcome eyesore who dared to brazenly walk past the monster on their porch and I felt exhausted. Grabbed several candles off the ledge and went back outside, where ancient horror at least didn't have the eyes to stare with.

Everything was still so I figured the talk has concluded. That was fast, but those two could probably slap one another with onslaught of information and be done.

I strode forward and began brazenly, "So, since I see you love the... Uh... Um. Am I interrupting...?"

I was, wasn't I? Fuck. Pressed on my eyes. I hated this weird place. I just wanted to go home, curl up in our living room to all the annoying chirping and never leave.

Priest was kneeling, forehead to the cobblestones, as though in a genuine worship. This instilled both fear and disgust in me. Was that my future? Was this what good pets did? Was this why the man had that completely spiritless look on his face? No wonder the others were bringing demon offerings - if even their leader treated this monstrosity so. Perhaps the government should bring the order back. Perhaps I should still burn myself alive and not risk bringing misfortune upon my house.

The demon walked off without a word and Priest stood up, looking at me. "He hates those," man said nodding towards candles as though that was the main thing to be addressed here.

"What, because of the fire?" I replied coolly, as if it was every day that I came across a cult leader prostrating himself before his god. I did stumble upon plenty of fucked up shit in my life, so it was a well-practised skill.

"They stink," Priest informed me and I nodded. Makes sense, I suppose. They did seem to have sensitive noses.

"That's even better!" I said cheerfully, as though we weren't on completely opposing sides on the scale of pleasing the demon. The cultist-in-chief didn't seem to mind. "Where'd he go?" I waved the candle in the air, wondering if I was free to go the other way.

"To kill them," Priest said simply.

One grovelling to take care of forty nuisances? I suppose it was worth it.

"Pretty ballsy. I've seen the military take down a lot of things."

Perhaps my woes were fleeting and this will all be over in ten minutes? Watching city defence at work was an understated pleasure of life. Monsters came in all shapes and sizes and displayed all kinds of unseen tricks, most of which seemed like magic in the eyes of children. Fuck, might have been exactly that because even as adult I had no explanation for most of them. And yet, bastion of humanity still stood.

"That's why I didn't go myself," Priest informed me unhelpfully.

"What does the monster want with this village anyway?" I asked instead of going down the road of thinking creature did this to help these people. His people?

"Nothing. It wouldn't care if every last one of them died."

Charming. I scrunched up my nose. "So, what? Because you asked?"

He sighed at the need to explain, "It's less of a hassle than putting me back together again, and then needing to go finish them off anyway."

I nodded empathetically. Must suck when runaway body parts keep getting into trouble. I shrugged that thought off and ended up hugging myself in the chill brought on by darkness. If the creature doesn't care for the people, what does it want with me?

Gunfire started crackling somewhere over the horizon. There was a lot of that incessant, dull noise. It didn't stop. I thought I heard screams, too, but perhaps that was just a vivid imagination. "Show off," Priest whispered, inclining the head to listen better. "All that ammo," he said regretfully, but there was no heart in it. Who in their right mind would complain about the things their very corporeal deity did?

"That doesn't sound like it's going smoothly," I commented sceptically to the obvious sounds of distress.

Dead eyes turned back at me with their own incredulity, intensifying explosions doing nothing to dissuade the fanatic. "They could have been dead without single one noticing," Priest spelled it out. I had to admit, he probably knew more than me.

"If it's so strong, why are the cities still standing?" I cut back, refusing to buy into the unseen things.

"Ash is not very interesting to play with," unblinking stare was hard to take when he particularly demanded it to be so. And it wasn't entirely pleasant to endure on a good day, either. Was I starting to rub this steadfast man wrong? About time.

"Hey," I called out holding that steely glare even though there was no reason to posture. He was a hardened gangster capable of many undesirable things and whilst I wouldn't be able to fight back, I thrived on general unwellness too. I guess I just wanted him to know. "What does it want with me?"

Priest looked away unexpectedly as though to concentrate on the sounds of waning gunfire. "For you to live." This discomf ort... the asshole knew something and deliberately hid it.

"He said he doesn't make people he'd just met into mouths. Is that where I'm headed?" I insisted.

"I don't know. Likely. Unnecessarily."

I grit my teeth. "What if I burn myself?"

The impassive eyes returned on me. "Probably too late for that now."

Well, fuck. Chewed on my lip. "You're obligated to say that. Even more than normal amount," I insisted.

Priest stared down at me still, his lips thinning some more. "Young man. Your only hope now is to become very dull." Oh, how I crave that. To just settle down on our beat-up couch and never move anymore.

"Is he a danger to the people I care about?"

"Are they interesting?" Was that supposed to be a joke? Either way, it just wasn't funny. Man who was dead on the inside was terrible at this, who knew?

I had nothing else to ask and plenty to ponder. Priest nodded a semblance of a goodbye and made himself scarce, probably to check up on the meat grinder caused by his deity because there was no path where he set off to. It was all quiet now. The devil must still be leisurely munching on the dead bodies.

Milton Keynes UK
Ingram Content Group UK Ltd.
UKHW021923151124
451262UK00014B/1567